DOMINANCE DELUSIONS

ALMA LAZAR

*This story is based on true facts.
All the names have been changed.*

Copyright©2024 Alma Lazar
All Rights Reserved
Library of Congress-TXu 2-420-608

To my beloved parents R.I.P.

*Thank you to my husband
who never stopped believing in me*

DOMINANCE DELUSIONS

ONE

"Mariana, is that you? The patient is sleeping now. Try to let her rest. You know she doesn't stop. The moment she has a small burst of energy, she starts doing things, and no one can stop her, and the doctor said she needs to rest."
"Is she still on a liquid diet?"

"On a very strict. The doctor mentioned that they could be weeks or months until we can start incorporating solids."

"Poor woman. I wouldn't know what to do if I needed to follow a liquid diet for three days."

"What would any person in her situation do? But she is different. She's made with a more resistant type of wood. She has the strength of an oak and the optimistic personality of a child. I don't get it."

"Neither could I imagine it. The things that we see in this work!

"I must run. It's my turn to pick my girl up at school. If you have any questions, call me on my cell."

"I think I heard some movement in the bedroom. I'm going to see if Mrs. Katya is waking up. I'll see you next time if we're assigned to the same patient."

"See you."

Still half asleep, trying to recognize voices, Katya asked.

"Is that you, Mariana?"

"Yes, Katya. They assigned me to this shift today. How do you feel?"

"BAD. I think I'm stepping foot in the land of dead. I wouldn't be surprised if the spirits come and take me soon."

"Don't say that. You still have a long way to go. I don't recall seeing any other patient with your strength, self-sufficiency, and desire to ignore the obstacles in your way."

"I am glad they assigned you to come today. I like it when you come. I love that reading interests you, and you keep me entertained when you read those books to me. And not only that, but you're organized, systematic, and like cleanliness, like me."

"Thank you. I also prefer to come here."

"I like it too when Mirna comes, but Mirna is not you. I prefer you. And the only thing I don't want is when they send Simon, the sour-faced, you don't get a smile from that man, even if you pay him. And if they are going to send me a male nurse, at least they should send me a young, handsome, and muscular with a well-defined round butt. Besides, Simon is not willing to share a single juicy gossip— one of those between nurses and doctors."

"Oh, Katya, you make me laugh with your sense of humor. Let me make your vitals routine check and ensure everything is fine. And after that, I will feed you some chicken broth. The doctor still hasn't authorized blended vegetables. Let's hope things will change soon, and you will see the delicious soups I will prepare for you. I have some healthy recipes that would be the envy of any chef."

"Any chef who likes to cook healthy, but I must inform you that 99.9% don't fit into that category. Maybe the chicken broth, I feel like it, but don't even mention the word vegetables to me now."

"Little by little, we will incorporate other stuff. The important thing here is that you eat whatever you want, even if it's not much. Eventually, we will change your diet so that you feel better and enjoy your meals. As soon as you finish your broth, we will read something. Last week, we finished the book THE HELP. Tell me which one you would like me to read now."

"What do you think about the book of Mariana?"

"Excuse me?"

"Yes, I would like to know about you. Why don't you tell me something, or better yet, everything about your life?"

Letting her gaze fall to the floor, Mariana replied. "I don't think you will be interested in what I can say. My life is not sophisticated like yours. It is I who is intrigued by your life. I would like to know the story behind those pictures that fill your wall from all your trips, I gather. So many interesting places in the world, especially that picture of the splendid sunset where the beautiful giraffe stands so proud above anyone else."

"Let's make a deal— we start with you today, and I promise to talk about myself he next time."

Mariana agreed, only to please Katya. After a stomach surgery of such magnitude, she thought it was best to give advantage to someone at a disadvantage, with the need of help 24 hours a day, without being able to eat anything else than what a strict diet would allow her, enduring pain so severe that could only be controlled by heavy doses of pain killers which the patient refused to take to prevent future addiction.

The actual circumstances of this patient were not pleasant— neither were the past circumstances in Mariana's life. Inside her, the demons were still on the loose. She'd carried a heavy weight on her shoulders. She had done it for a long time, the same way she'd been doing with her powerlessness, her rage, and her hopelessness. But perhaps it was time to reveal her past, especially to this person she felt identified with, this lady with whom she liked to have those prolonged conversations and who probably didn't have too much time left to live.

With a profound inhale, like someone who prepares to start walking on fire with bare feet, with a soft voice, Mariana said—

"I'm going to tell you my story as it is, but I will need to start way back in time, even before I was born."

Without thinking, in an instant, Mariana was revealing that naked truth adhered to her, the truth she tried unsuccessfully to get rid of for a long time, that truth that haunted and asphyxiated her, that made her feel victim and sometimes guilty without having a valid reason. Wanting to vent the secrets kept for so long, she started narrating the details she knew of since before her birth.

Susana, her mother, worked for a war veteran in Los Angeles. She took care of the house cleaning. And there, she met Jimmy, the gardener. They were close friends, and the friendship became a physical attraction, at least on Jimmy's side, who was 29 years older than her. But Jimmy was a good man with a wife and two sons, and he did everything possible to prevent the physical attraction in that relationship from growing.

On the other hand, he knew he had no chance of competing with his boss—a handsome, rich American man with all the experience that a man of words, 43 years older, could have to make women fall into his nets. After a few months, Susana was expecting her boss' baby without realizing when it happened and without being able to prevent it.

Going deep into details would be unnecessary, but on her 32nd week of pregnancy, Susana was deported to Mexico, her country of origin.

Not long after, Jimmy, tired of the sun, the pesticides, the back pains, and being old enough to retire, decided to go back to Tijuana, Mexico, where occasionally, he did independent gardening jobs. His income was not even a shadow of what it had been in the

United States, but being smart and organized, he invested in a small property to live in with his family. At the same time, he could keep a small and modest house where he used to live before, in an area rather dangerous than humble, but that's what he had and opted to help Susana, renting her that small house at a lower price than its value, securing a roof for her and her daughter.

The memory of Mariana didn't go beyond her six years of age. Perhaps because that marked the beginning of her misfortune or because it marked the awakening of her destiny, but this is what she recalls from her childhood—

"Kid, can you walk faster?"

"No, Mom, I can't. These shoes are too tight. And here, there's mud all over. It's hard for me to walk."

"I'm sorry, princess. I will speak with the governor tomorrow so that they make a new street for you to walk comfortably."

"Really?"

"Of course not, silly. And hurry up. I'm getting tired of you. Don't you see those weird men walking in our direction? For sure, they're not up to anything good."

"I'm scared, Mom."

"Me too, but in the next corner is Don Chema's furniture factory. Those bullies are only brave when they see women alone. As soon as they see men around, I assure you, they will walk away."

"Yes, Mom, let's go. There's somebody outside."

"Good afternoon, Don Chema. Could we wait here for a moment while the scoundrels go away? They come very close to us."

"Those scoundrels again? It would help if we had lights on the streets and if, once in a while, the patrol cars would show up around here."

"The gangs in this barrio multiply like plagues. It's either the ones making drugs, the bums getting drunk, or the assailants. And not to mention the rapists. But the government keeps pretending that nothing is going on. How easy for them since none of them live around here. Oh! But wait till the elections come close because then you will see candidates from all parties offering heaven and earth and promising that everything will change once they are elected. As if we were not sick of listening to their broken record so many times."

When the bullies passed next to Susana, one of them made a sign with his tongue, provoking her repugnance— but that's a common thing among the men of this barrio, especially when more than two get together. Another gang member celebrated this gesture as a heroic action, thinking that the next time, they would get their way.

For the first time that evening, in that uncomfortable house where they lived, Mariana felt protected— they were safe, and the gang was nowhere to be seen. Inside that place, no one would know there were three helpless women— besides Mariana, her mother, and her grandmother lived there.

"Mom, why don't we move to another place? I don't like living here."

"Do you have any idea about how expensive the rents are? I can hardly pay Jimmy what he's charging me. And you're telling me you want to move? I think you're crazy. But if you feel uncomfortable, I already have a solution."

"Which one?"

"One lady is going to adopt you. She is your aunt's sister."

"The sister of which aunt?"

"My brother's wife's sister."

"But we never see them, and I don't even know that lady. Are my grandma and you too coming with me?"

"No. It will be only you. It's been a while since that lady wanted to adopt you. She will take good care of you, and you will also live in a house better than this. Besides, I have Eustolio in my life now. Your grandma and I can move to his house, but it would be only the two of us because two is already a squad."

"I don't like that man. I hate that you two drink alcohol when he's here, and then start fighting. Besides, he acts weird. I want Jimmy instead. With him, I would go, but I want you and my grandma to come with me."

"So, you think that you can choose my partner? I'm fine with Eustolio. He's the one I want to be with, and Jimmy wouldn't take you with him because his wife is sick. Jimmy says she doesn't have much time to live, and he needs to take care of her."

"I don't want to go, Mommy. Please! Let me stay here with you."

"It is decided. They will come to pick you up tomorrow around noon."

TWO

The following morning, my mom bathed me and fixed me up in my favorite dress— a yellow and white dress that the Sisters from *The House of the Poor* had given me the day of the Santos Reyes. She braided my hair, put a purple bow on it, and cleaned my shoes. I don't know if she did it for me to keep a good memory of my last day at home or to impress the lady who would later take me with her in adoption. My mom had just finished doing my hair when they knocked at the door. It surprised us to see Eustolio that early and sober. He used to come at night after work and was usually drunk. He had a pretty pinwheel in his hand— "Look what I got you," he said, "it spins with the wind, and when there's no wind, you can spin it with your finger. Go outside and play with it while I talk to your mom."

"Don't get your shoes dirty," my mom added.

From a distance, I could see that they were talking, and sometimes it seemed like they were arguing.

"Are they coming to pick up the girl today?"

"Yes. They'll be here soon, probably before lunch."

"Are you sure about what you're doing? Think that once

she's gone, you won't see her again, and I believe that a woman belongs with her children— what if later I lose the respect for you for what you did? Besides, that is the only child you have. Think about what would happen if we decide to get married in the future and you can't have more children. The kid is not bad. And once she grows up, she can help you, especially when you get old. You will need her to take care of you. Look at your mother. What would she do without you?"

Eustolio and my mom talked for a long time, and after, she called me and told me to get in. "I'm going to change your dress. You're not going anywhere. You'll stay with us."

It's still raining, and I want the sun to come out so that I can go out and play with my friend Karina. I don't like to be in this house. It's cold, and I don't want to be here, mainly when my grandma is not here. I don't like to be with her either. She's always drinking, and when my mom gets home, they fight. My mom tells her not to leave the house because she needs to watch over me. I'm already six years old. I don't need anybody to watch over me. Grandma Inés never plays with me. She only drinks, so when she leaves, I'm OK. She always says that she won't take long and that she's only going out to buy her medicine, but she leaves for many hours and returns with a bottle. That's not medicine. That's what she drinks to get drunk.

My mom says that my grandma begs to get money for her beer. Sometimes, she returns with a bottle of something that looks like water but is not. They don't allow me to drink it because it's alcohol, and I can get sick. I believe my mom doesn't love my grandma. She is mean to her and says that Grandma is worthless— I think she is waiting for her to die. I'm not sure I love her either. I only hear her argue and fight, but I don't like that Mom treats her like that and tells me to throw stones at her. I don't know if that is right. It makes me feel bad. I feel sad for her. I wish I hadn't listened to my mom that day when she convinced me to throw a stone at my grandma. I didn't want to do it, but Mom insisted, saying that Grandma was used to it and it didn't hurt her since she never learned her lessons. I believe I made a deep wound on her head, and she was bleeding, and I cried thinking I killed her. I don't want to kill my grandma.

"Mariana, I'm going out for a moment to buy my medicine. Don't leave the house until I come back."
OK, grandma. I will only talk through the window with my friend Kary if she passes by."

Three hours waiting for somebody to have pity on me, a coin here and there doesn't help much, but at least it's something.
"Here, señora." A North American man told Inés in perfect Spanish, giving her a ten-dollar bill.
And I didn't believe in miracles! Without a doubt, this is my lucky day. But the gringo wasn't willing to leave without giving me a lecture first.
"This is your pass for a better life. Don't spend it on alcohol. Go and get yourself something to eat, something you're craving and haven't eaten in a long time. Enjoy it and take the opportunity to reflect because the road to alcohol doesn't lead to anything good— your best thing to do is to stay away. And you will discover there are countless things in life worth living. All you need to do is ask for help, and you will be surprised by all the people you can't even imagine that are willing to help you."
This is not what I had in mind for today. But what if the gringo is right? Maybe if I manage to stay sober for a few days, I can go back to work sweeping floors in offices like I used to,

I can get myself some tacos, and I'll still have some money left, perhaps at the swap meet I could even buy a toy or a t-shirt for Mariana.

"Hey, you old boozer." The scoundrels told Inés as they got close to her. "Are you still sober? It's almost 3 p.m., and you're still not wasted? What's the matter? Wasn't business good today?"

"Leave me alone, bastards, you bunch of bums. You had to be working instead of trying to rob a poor old woman like me, but you're wasting your time. You know I don't have a penny on me."

"Oh yeah? What about the bill the gringo gave you. Did you hide it in your round, gorgeous boobs, or we made a mistake, and you ate it?"

"Bunch of idiots. It was just a paper that fell on the floor, and I bent down to pick it up."

"A paper? Then the güero wants to take you to dinner and gave you his phone number."

Cracking into a mocking laugh, the three bums pushed Inés in different directions, searching her fragile body until they could get the bill, leaving her on the floor. Triumphant with their cowardly action before they started running, they all hit the woman with fists and feet, leaving her on the floor with a bloody face and no money.

"This will teach you to not try to make fools of us the next time you have a hidden little bill on you."

Grandma is taking too long. She should be here by now. It's still a few hours before my mom gets off work— my friend Kary passed by in the morning, but it's been a while, and I would like her to come because lately, Eustolio has been coming earlier, and I feel uncomfortable when he's here. I don't want him to be here, especially when he knows my mom is not in the house. The good thing is that grandma is always around, but.... What if something happened to her today? It's still a long time before my mom comes back. And as soon as it gets dark, Kary's parents don't let her go out. Now that the weather is getting colder, it gets dark earlier, and I don't know how to close the door so Eustolio won't come in, but he's going to knock, and I will have to open. He knows my mom doesn't take me with her when she's selling candy. I pray that my mom is having a good day today and that she finishes early and comes soon— hopefully, Eustolio won't come drunk tonight.

The loud knocking on the door scared me. It seemed like somebody wanted to bring it down. My heart pounded so hard it felt like it would explode just imagining Eustolio drunk outside. I managed to distinguish the figure of my grandma, through the gaps in the wooden door. I hurriedly opened the door, and it surprised me to see her with a bloody face.

"Grandma, what happened to you?"

"Those bastards attacked me in the street. Silly of me! I thought that I'd had a good day because a man gave me ten dollars "to buy some food," he said. And I thought about bringing some tacos, but I thought about it too long, and those sons of a *#$%* attacked me."

"Grandma, what do we do? Do I see if Kary's dad is at home? Or do I tell the other neighbors to come and help us?"

"You know the neighbors don't see us with good eyes, nobody wants us in this barrio, they are always complaining if we fight, if we drink or if we make noise, we are the stinky ones of this neighborhood, and Kary's dad hasn't come back from work yet."

"Then, what do I do? Your face is bleeding. Why don't you go and rinse it?"

"Rinse it? Do you have any idea how bad it hurts me? Of course you don't. You don't have any idea of anything. You live in limbo. The time will come when you grow up, and you will start learning, then you will realize that the only remedy for all ills is alcohol."

"Alcohol takes the pain away?"

"It doesn't, but it helps to forget. You drink till you fall unconscious, and then you feel no pain in the body or the soul. You only drink until you feel you start to float, like a leaf that suddenly falls to the ground, and afterward, everybody will step on it."

"And now, without alcohol, will your face hurt until Mom comes home?"

"Give me some of those pills your mom takes for her headaches. Bring me three and a soda. And if we don't have soda, bring me water.

At six years old, if I could've had the wisdom that time as it passes leaves us, I would've had solutions for all the difficult moments that I faced alone, but at that age, we don't have wisdom— we only have that children insecurity, the need of protection, of love, of having adults around us with answers to all of our questions and solutions to all the problems. However, most of the time by myself, I learned to face the challenge with courage. I was getting ahead with the body and soul of a little girl and the responsibility of an adult.

Listening to the muffled steps approaching the door, fear took over me. Those were not the familiar, hurried steps of my mom— those were heavier, they were the steps of a man who terrified me. That feeling that started as mistrust grew with time to become fear, insecurity, and desire without knowing why to hide or run away every time Eustolio was around, but that was the man my mom had chosen to spend the nights with, to forget her loneliness and with the hope to have a man that made her feel she was not alone, even though her loneliness was already an inherent part of her.

THREE

A few days after the adoption issue was left behind, Eustolio convinced my mom to move in with him. He lived close to our house, and it was convenient for my mom to save some money in rent, share the expenses with her partner, and, at the same time, live with the man she thought she was in love with.

Jimmy didn't like the idea when my mom told him about her plans. Mainly because his wife had already passed away and he had something else in mind regarding my mom, but he always supported her morally and even financially when she went through rough times, whether she was on her own or had someone else in her life, Jimmy was always there for her.

One afternoon, I saw the sparkle in Grandma's eyes when Eustolio came home with a bottle of tequila in his hand.

"Come here, doña Ines," he told my grandma, tapping on the chair next to him, "let's have a shot while we wait for Susana."

I remember how full those shots were, all to the brim. The tequila was going down with inexplicable speed, and he forced my grandma to drink faster every time. In the blink of an eye, she fell asleep on the table.

Five minutes passed or maybe less, and, with clear evidence, I couldn't hide my fear when Eustolio grabbed me by the shoulder and took me to the sofa, asking me to sit next to him.

"Don't be afraid, child. I won't harm you. Don't you know that I love you as a father would?"

He said, while he kept pulling me tighter to his body. The confusion, the fear of being alone with him, and the repugnant smell of alcohol from his mouth have remained embedded in my memory. But destiny, which on one side is cruel, takes away what we love the most and beats us where it most hurts, and on its opposite component, helps us to survive and take away memories, for if they remain in our minds, would not let us live in peace, so I don't recall details of how things happened. All I remember is that I cried inconsolably in one corner, and when my mom got home, I told her I had a sore throat and went to bed.

I felt like I lost everything that evening— not only my innocence and my childhood, but also my joy for life. I couldn't understand what I had experienced. I wondered if all the girls go through that when there's no father around to protect and guide them. I also asked myself if all men are that evil. And I thought about my mother and grandmother and if they also had to go through the same as children, if all women come to this world only to suffer since childhood, and if we are condemned to be an instrument for men's pleasure. They make me sick.

As time passed, fear and hate— if it's possible for a child at that age to hate, took over me. I felt immeasurable anger at Eustolio and also blamed my mother for making us live under the same roof as that man who came to destroy all my dreams and stole in such a manner my joy, my unconcern, and my childish behavior.

For many years, I regretted the day that the lady who wanted to adopt me went to pick me up, and I wished something would happen to stop me from leaving my house and my mom. How little did I know about the intentions of that despicable man who convinced my mother not to give me up for adoption because that didn't fit in his perverse game.

Several days passed and I felt consumed by fear. I was desperate to tell my mom, but I dreaded her reaction. I didn't want her to get mad at me. She was all I had. Even if we never had a loving or perfect relationship, she was still my mother, the only person that, at least in a limited way, had protected me since my childhood— she and my grandmother during her sober moments, and ashamed of myself I kept quiet but that perverted man seeing that I still carried my secret decided to repeat his infamous sin.

More than once, I was a victim of abuse, but the day came when I couldn't keep the secret any longer and revealed it to my friend Kary. We hugged and cried together. The explosion of feelings couldn't pass unnoticed by her mom. And I had no choice but to reveal the facts that had kept asphyxiating me for some time.

Taking me by the hand, the lady directed us to my mom. It was the moment of truth, and I shared all the details as far back as my memory could reach. My mom was furious. Not with me as I'd imagined, but with Eustolio. That night, she confronted him. Of course, he insisted that I was lying. But a mother knows—she knew that the man she trusted, thinking he would be by her side to love and cherish her, was using her to satisfy his detestable libido with mother and daughter and take advantage of a helpless child.

"I promise you. That miserable man won't ever touch you once more." My mother told me after knowing about the reprehensible events. "I will make sure this won't ever happen again."

The day after, she took me with her to work, but before, we stopped by Jimmy's place. There, my mom and he talked for a while. I lost track of how long it was, but it was a long time. After we left, my mom said our lives would change with Jimmy's help.

Ever since that day, my mom never lost sight of me. She took me to her work and always watched over me when we were in the house.

One night, when Eustolio, drunk to his ears, started to snore and it seemed as if not even an earthquake could wake him up, my mom started to fill a burgundy suitcase with as much as she could. Trying not to make any noise, she, my grandma, and I left the house.

We walked and passed perhaps two or three bus stops until we took the right bus. Approximately one hour later, we got off in the middle of the road. The night was quiet and cold, the darkness extreme, and the silence deep— the only thing we could see several steps ahead was a light bulb outside a small grocery store. We directed toward the light. It was late, I suppose after midnight, and we were the only ones there. My mom and my grandma were frightened. On the other hand, I was not scared for the first time in a long time. Something inside told me we would be fine, and I tried to convince them they shouldn't be afraid either.

I don't know how long we waited until we took the next bus. As we arrived in Tecate, Jimmy was at the bus station waiting for us. At that moment, I imagined I was seeing an angel. He took us to his tiny little house. That night, he slept on the floor, my grandma on the sofa, and my mom and I in his bedroom.

The day after, he took us to a hill where he bought a compact piece of land and was building a little blue house made of steel or aluminum, something like a trailer.

"It will soon be ready, and we'll all move in here," he told my mom. "In the meantime, I will take you to my compadre Elias' workshop. It is a big place with a spacious warehouse, mostly empty. I will buy some folding beds to use later in the house. My compadre says that if you wish, you can stay there until the house is finished."

We were there for some time. Everyone treated us well. They appreciated Jimmy and felt happy to be able to give him a hand. When he finished building the little blue house, we moved in. It was at the beginning of winter— I remember it being frigid in winter and hot during the summer. And when it rained in December or January, due to the aluminum in the house, the rain seemed to tear from the cold and the noise hammering every inch of the roof. But there, I felt happy and safe. Jimmy loved me and treated me as a daughter. To me, he was the father that I never had. I didn't know this until a few years later, but since the day of my birth, he registered me and gave me his last name. Since I knew about that, he was always my Papa Jimmy. It was he who saved me and gave meaning to my life.

Gradually, that favorable change helped me to fade away the horrors of my previous years. My mom also changed. She quit drinking for some time and had peace next to my Papa Jimmy. We all had peace in our lives, but despite his efforts to give us the best of the little he had, he also used to drink— he wasn't violent like Eustolio was and never dared to hurt my mom. Nevertheless, alcohol changes human beings, whether they are violent or peaceful, as they end up in a modified behavior, and where there is some hidden resentment, those feelings surface.

As to Mom, I don't think she ever was in love with Papa Jimmy. He was 29 years older than her. I believe she mostly saw him as a paternal figure. She liked the feeling of being protected and safe. But if someone else crossed her path by the fortunes of destiny, she didn't hesitate to delude herself into thinking she'd found the ideal man and that my Papa Jimmy would be willing to accept her small infidelities. However, he felt deeply hurt, and the arguments surfaced under the heat of alcohol.

FOUR

Being a family and living as such, made the four of us happy, to the possible extent of happiness according to our bitter past. My life experienced a remarkable change. They no longer tied me, and the beatings I was exposed to when Eustolio and my mom were together were left behind. Papa Jimmy and I were the happiest.

In the chest of my childhood memories, the ones that by a personal decision I wanted not only to keep but imprison for them not to escape my mind, stood up the day when my Papa Jimmy took me to a place called Cañada Verde, a gorgeous park with the fresh scent of a spring morning and countless trees in all shapes and sizes for as far as the sight could reach. There were also stables and cattle— lots of cows and horses. Near that place, a friend of my dad owned a bicycle shop. We made our first stop there, and, to my surprise, my dad bought me a bicycle before continuing to Cañada Verde, where he was teaching me how to ride it since that was my first time in such an activity.

From the scant happy memories of my childhood, this is worth it for all of them. Being surrounded by all of those trees in the middle of that comforting and vast green area, having the immense privilege of a healthy interaction between father and daughter, but mainly, that moment when my dad released the bicycle for me to continue on my own— it was the happiest moment of my short existence. I felt like I was flying and experienced that sense of freedom. Mostly, I was giving my Papa Jimmy a reason to be proud of me. I'd overcome fear and had passed the test. I could ride a bicycle without the need for anyone to hold me.

As I felt more confident, I increased my speed. Suddenly, one boy passed near me without holding the handlebar, and I did not hesitate to imitate him. I waited to be close to my Papa Jimmy. I still don't know if I did it to feel safe, in case I would fall, or to show off my progress on this new adventure. He yelled at me with fear rather than feeling pride— "Mariana, don't let go of the handlebar." With evident sadness, I had no option but to obey. Through time, I understood that we can't run without first learning to walk. Life has different stages, and whether we approve of them or not, we need to give each of them its place.

It seemed time flew on that morning. A personal perception of paradise varies according to each human being— to me, being in that place was like paradise, and if the birds communicate with children, in my little girl's mind, I felt like it was me whom they talked to, I later learned that they communicate with each other. I had that vivid memory of how the happy birds chirped from branch to branch, and I tried to understand what they wanted to tell me, however, their joyful conversation, had nothing to do with me— they were only enjoying those moments of freedom the same way I was, contemplating all of those beautiful trails, with the hues of green from the trees treating us to serenity and peace, as well as with an infinite sensation of wellbeing. From far away, they seemed to blend with the sky to become a giant sphere that enveloped me in my private world, which I never wanted to leave.

My happiness started to fade as the majestic blue of the sky slowly turned gray.

"Mariana, we have to go before it starts to rain."

With indescribable sadness, I didn't want my Papa Jimmy to see me cry. I didn't want to throw a tantrum since I was not that type of child. Nonetheless, I could not stop a silent tear from rolling down my cheek.

"What do you think if we sit for a few minutes on the roofed bench? Come, bring your bicycle. Let's sit and wait until the clouds disappear, but if it rains, we will go. Do you agree?"

We had just sat on the bench when I felt the first thick and heavy raindrops. The pain in my heart could not have been sharper. I could have continued playing in the rain, but it was not up to me.

"We will wait a little bit until the rain stops, and then we leave." My Papa Jimmy said, and I agreed, knowing there was no point in objecting, but destiny seemed to be on my side. Not long after, the rain suddenly stopped, and the sun started to come out. If miracles exist, I can assure you that on that day, one took place. A rainbow appeared after the sun. I had never seen a rainbow before. Puzzled, I asked my dad what had just happened. "Is the rainbow," he answered.

"What is a rainbow?"

"It's a gift from nature. Sometimes, she feels guilty for interrupting activities that we would not like to come to an end. As compensation, it delights us with that beautiful color display."

"Why isn't there a rainbow where we live?"

"There is. The rainbow is everywhere. Although we can't see it all the time, it comes out after the rain when the sun suddenly appears, and today, it showed up to leave you with a beautiful memory."

"And now that the sun is out, can we stay a little longer?"

"Only for a bit. But you won't be able to ride your bike for now because there's mud, and you might slip. We will return another day with your mom so she can see how well you learned to ride the bike."

It was hard for me to leave that place at the time to return home. I would've loved to stay there forever. I imagined I wanted to live in a place like that when I grew up. If there's a point where dreams come true, that day in that place was the cusp of mine. I've always been grateful for those moments of happiness that will remain in me for the rest of my days.

My childhood continued, casual and happy. My fears were vanishing, and my dad decided to provide me with an education. He was talking about sending me to school so I could learn to write and read and coexist with other children. I couldn't have felt happier every time they talked about it, and I asked Grandma when she was at home to start teaching me to write the first letters.

In the meantime, my dad bought me a notebook and a pencil and went ahead with the teaching process— but more than the school education, he focused on family values that only parents can teach.

On one occasion, my mom brought home more money than usual. The sales had been good that day, she said. I couldn't resist the temptation when I saw her coming with all that money, and I sneaked into her purse when she got distracted and took a ten-dollar bill.

I managed to stop by a neighbor's house who was three years older than me and asked her to go with me to a candy stand nearby, where we bought as much candy as that bill allowed us. That day I felt I was living the chapter of a fairy tale with all that candy, which, in my mind, belonged to me. But nothing falls from the sky, let alone when it was acquired with someone else's work and without their consent.

When I got home with my treasure and with my neighbor, my Papa Jimmy asked me where the money for all that candy came from. That gave me an indefinable knot in my stomach, and I had to tell him the truth. The anxiety reflected on his face came without warning, but he didn't dare to touch me or raise his voice— he only told my friend not to hang out with me because I was a thief.

Anguished and baffled, I woke up to reality to learn since that age the consequence of stealing— trying to justify my unnecessary act, I couldn't find a reason to believe that what I'd done was a childhood mischief for that was not a child's action, to steal is a baseness that only adults without conscious are capable of.

I felt ashamed after my lie was exposed, and the morning after, not only did I try to avoid my friend, but I wanted to run away from my Papa Jimmy, who said that there was no reason for my mom to know about that incident, but he was willing to be my accomplice only for that one time since the first time is a mistake, but a second one would be a vice not acceptable in our house.

Frequently, things hadn't gone my way. Unease, I was afraid that my Papa Jimmy could stop loving me for what I did, but his heart and the wisdom that comes only with age were huge. He opted for leaving things behind sooner than I thought. Through his noble behavior, he left me with a valuable lesson. If I was ashamed to imagine that my dad would see me with lower esteem, I also learned something else on that day, and I can proudly say that from then on, I never repeated a steal for as insignificant or justified as it might seem.

FIVE

After a long talk between my mom and my Papa Jimmy in which they allowed me to participate, even though my opinion rights were limited, at least I could listen. And I recalled feeling important and happy. My dad decided I was old enough to start going to school. Although most kids cry, imagining they will separate from their moms for a few hours, I, on the contrary, felt excitement. Perhaps I wasn't that young and had passed that stage when children start going to pre-school, usually to play and prepare themselves to socialize and understand that if humans can compare to birds, one day the time will come to fly away from the nest.

Like most low-income people, I couldn't afford the luxury of going to pre-school and, a couple of years later, participating in a graduation ceremony with the whole family attendance, followed by a celebration as if it was a medical career or any other defining the future of the graduate. That's for wealthy families. I went directly to the first year of elementary.

It excited me to go to school. I was restless and wanted to play with other children, but it was not only that. I liked to learn. It motivated me to start writing and reading my first words. I was discovering a new world, but this new world of mine, up to a certain point, complicated my parents' lives since we lived far from the school. Looking for a practical solution, they decided I should move and spend the weekdays at the girls' house. I don't recall the names of any of them. All I remember is that those were the girls I used to play with, while living in the warehouse. They kindly offered me lodging since they lived close to school, and it was convenient for my mom and my Papa Jimmy. I spent there Monday through Friday, and on Friday afternoons, they would pick me up and take me back home.

When I said that I didn't remember the girls' names, it was because maybe my mind decided to erase certain undesired circumstances from my childhood. I neither remember the parents' names. And now that I think about it, I owe it to my survival instinct, the motor of the human mechanism. We decide to forget, leave the past behind, and concentrate on the future, for the hope of the future keeps us alive.

I spent happy moments in that house where they welcomed and treated me well. I played with the girls, and their mom treated me with some consideration. She was kind to me and watched over me as she did with her children. She saw me as one of them, and the father also treated me well, or at least at the beginning, until one day, the same thing that happened with Eustolio before was repeated. I was eight years old then. I didn't know what type of body I had or what it looked like at that age— the only thing I'm positive of is that I still was a child with the same casual attitude and the insecurity of a helpless child, as most children are. I don't understand how adults with lustful desires and limitless evilness can achieve their nefarious intentions. In that house, there were usually the girls, their parents, and me, but that one time, when the innocence that slowly started to return to my life was stolen again, we were only that man and me.

DOMINANCE DELUSIONS

I was plagued with rage and repugnance but mainly ashamed. I did not want my Papa Jimmy to find out. This time, however, I was not willing to carry a pang of guilt without being guilty. So that weekend, when my parents picked me up, as soon as we got home, I talked to my mom and told her that I did not have intentions, nor did I want to return to that family's house. I remember I cried for a long time and asked my mom to keep it from my dad. Uncontrollably furious, although trying hard not to give my dad the full details, my mom wanted him to know what kind of person his so-called friend was. My Papa Jimmy loved me dearly, and we feared a violent reaction, so trying to sugarcoat the facts, my mom said that I did not want to go to that house anymore because his friend made me feel uncomfortable with the way he looked at me.

To my dad, that was an adequate reason for not ever letting me go back to that house, and, although I wasn't old enough to ride the bus by myself, trying to solve the situation, my mom suggested that the bus would be our best option for my transportation and using her usual convincing technique, she told my dad— "Mariana can take the bus at the corner outside the school, even when it takes a long time to get here, you can calculate the arriving time and can pick her up at the bus stop."

On my first Monday riding the bus, I was happy. It was an adventure. Being alone made me feel important. I felt like a grown-up person, and I enjoyed those commutes to and from school. Above all, I loved seeing myself surrounded by people— the more packed the bus was, the better for me. In those moments, I was not alone. I was at peace, imagining that no one could hurt me.

Now that I look back, I see it absurd to think someone could feel happy commuting on an overloaded bus. Sometimes, when driving, I look at the buses next to me, especially the full ones. I see the people inside, and I try to imagine where they are heading to, how they live, if they are not in a hurry to arrive at their destination, and what thoughts cross their minds when they commute with that heavy traffic. And I ask myself if some of those have a vehicle and on that day, they saw themselves in need to service it and took public transportation.

I continued riding the bus to school and liked it more each time. Not only did I like riding the bus, but I also loved attending school. Besides Karina, I had three other friends— Rosita, Selena, and Malú. At times, I also saw the girls from the house where I previously lived, the two older ones, the youngest did not have the age yet to attend school. And if these girls once were my first friends in Tecate when I lived in the warehouse, later we grew apart— they went to the same school as me, but since they were older, we were not in the same classrooms.

Now and then, we used to say hi when we saw each other. But for me, it was essential to forget those days I spent in their house. I have nothing against those girls. They were children, the same as me, and I'm positive they never knew about their father's despicable act. As for their mother, I don't know either if one day she found out and she acted as she didn't, like certain women sometimes do, despite being hurt or humiliated or discovering that dirty side in their partners and opting to ignore and forget for fear of losing the man they live with.

It is hard for me to describe the way I felt living in the little blue house— it was cold and small, not to mention the location in a dangerous area, but to an eight-year-old girl, it was not easy to measure danger, and I felt safe arriving home and seeing my Papa Jimmy. It was a well-being sensation that kept me from fear. When he was not at home, and my mom was out working, I was not afraid either— my dad had already trained us to defend ourselves in case one day we would need to. Since I stopped going back to the girls' house, despite never knowing what happened, he had a gut feeling that he should exercise uninterrupted over-protection on my mom, my grandma, and above all, me. And he did it in every possible way.

I tried to live normally, if it was possible for an eight-year-old girl abused by two different men to live that way. I felt like the times of abuse were left behind. And that they would never be repeated. I continued going to school, and I loved it. I liked the learning part and seeing my friends every day. Of the three, Malú was the only one without a father. Selena continuously showed up at school with bruises all over— her parents used to drink and abused her frequently. Rosita was never abused, but at her house there was a family situation that dragged her into rebellious behavior. My Papa Jimmy, on Saturdays or Sundays, used to take me to play in the park where I knew I would see Malú since she lived close by.

At the age of eleven, inexplicably, I was abused for the third time, except that on that day, things happened differently. On that occasion, I could say the abuse was partial— the person in question, my neighbor, touched my body, but at least then, I didn't experience the previous repulsion of the abuse between an adult and a child. He was nineteen years old, not considered a mature adult yet. He had the advantage of not being a man old enough to be my father. Mostly, what I felt that day was regret that has haunted me since then.

For the first time, and to my surprise, I didn't feel sick to my stomach, nor did I have the panic experienced previously. This time, I am almost positive I was enjoying it, and that's what makes me feel bad, carrying the heavy remorse and asking myself if I ever provoked the situation because I still don't understand how someone would dare to do something like that. On this occasion, though, I acted differently because the feeling of disgust was not there. This time, unlike before, I stayed quiet when he touched certain parts of my body, awakening a new sensation because the physical feeling was dissimilar.

SIX

"Katya, it is your turn to talk about your life. Enough of my tragedies already. Let's switch to something more pleasant. What do you think if now you talk about yourself?"

"Oh, dear, I don't know. After everything you've been through, it might be unwise to talk about me. And trust me. There were times that I thought I had it hard, but after listening to what you narrated, I'm under the impression I've been on a bed of roses. But in the end, there is no such thing as a perfect life, and suffering is a familiar road for everyone— for some, it is extreme, and for others, it comes on waves of a minor frequency, but no one escapes from it."

Feeling guilty about how Katya lived or what she'd achieved and accumulated through her existence, she returned to her childhood.

I was born and lived my childhood and most of my adolescence in a small town with rivers, lakes, and waterfalls in Missouri, with a population of not more than 30,000. I was always a popular girl but not among the girls at school or my neighbors— mostly, it was among guys who saw me as a tomboy type as I chose to run, climb trees, and play baseball, while the other girls preferred to play with dolls. But above all, I was always an animal lover.

For my 6th birthday, my mom, who was more excited than me, organized a party and invited all my classmates. There were lots of pink and lavender balloons and a sizable cake inspired by a Disney theme, and to her surprise, she discovered that the attendants were boys, on the whole.

"Where are all your girl classmates?" She asked.

"I don't think they will come. They don't like to get their dress dirty when they play. They prefer to play with barbies, and I find that boring. But at least my friend Sandy showed up. She always likes to spend time with me— she can play with dolls, ride bikes, or play hide and seek and has fun while playing with me, and if she's here, I don't need any other girl to come."

At first, the boys gave me a hard time. I beat some of them jogging, and they didn't like it. Suddenly, they started bullying me for being one of the shortest in class. One day, they wanted to take me for their little pig, especially Jerry. I don't know why he disliked me, but he went too far with his jokes and said I wasn't tall enough to win a jogging competition. He asked me if I was cheating or how I managed to beat some of them.

"I'll show you how," I said, and without thinking, I threw him a punch that left him with a flying tooth. I don't think my punch was so strong. Most likely, his tooth was already loose, and circumstances favored me. From that day on, I believe I established my territory. No one ever bullied me again. On the contrary, my popularity grew since Jerry was not a boy who stand out for his likable personality or physical appearance, and most of the boys were leaning to my side, especially the friends of my youngest brother Güicho.

I am sure Sandy felt embarrassed by the smack incident, but to a certain point, she felt protected by me despite her being three inches taller.

A few years later, and not long after my tenth birthday, my parents took Güicho, my sister Amanda, my friend Sandy, our dog Peluchin, and me to the 4th of July picnic. My dad had a red Volkswagen van with a white or beige roof. Over time, when I learned something about art, one day in our garage, I found an old calendar with a Norman Rockwell illustration called Coming and Going. Since his paintings and drawings were inspired by everyday life scenes, it gave me the impression that our 4th of July picnic was his source of inspiration for the Coming and Going painting, which, some years later, would become one of his classic works.

The day of the picnic was unforgettable for a reason. That evening, when the sun was setting, I said I was going to the restroom the moment I saw my friend Sergio going down the steps. We talked under the stands for a while, and suddenly, he kissed me. On that 4th of July, I felt like I was touching the sky. I thought I was in love for the first time. Sergio kissed me on the cheek, and then he started running. I spent days wishing it would happen again. My multiple attempts to meet alone proved unsuccessful. It was the beginning of summer vacation, and most of the time, our parents and other kids were around when we met. At the end of the summer, I found out that Sergio's father was transferred from his work to Virginia Beach, taking his family with him, and that was the end of my first love.

I finished elementary school always involved in sports activities. I liked volleyball, but I didn't qualify to belong to the school team due to my short stature, and I had to spend a couple of years playing softball. Afterward, I started high school, and by then, I had friends— female friends, but Sandy kept on being the closest one. There were four of us in the group, and we all were cheerleaders of The Red Knights, our school's football team. Every Friday and Saturday, we had parties. And on Sundays, most of the time, we had picnics. It was prohibited for the boys to attend the parties on a Friday because they had to practice at night, and later, they needed to rest for the games on Saturdays, but sometimes they managed to show up at the parties.

Corina, one of the girls in the group, had a car, and when there was not much action at the Friday parties, we went to the outdoor movie theater, which fascinated me. Although I preferred the cinema to the parties, I had to go where most of them wanted. Sometimes, we got in trouble, the kind of troubles from the '50s, those that you didn't get to see, and if we compare those to the ones from present times, we conclude that back in those days, there were no troubles.

Going back to my childhood remote times and the first years of my youth, I can assure you it was a quiet life. I could describe it as happy. Back then, both of my parents lived, and although they sometimes argued because of my mom's strict beliefs in disciplining my siblings and me, we did not experience severe family problems. We lived in that happy atmosphere of the small cities with a population so small that all the families knew and were close to each other. Businesses, regardless of their type, were prosperous. Overall, there was only one of each genre, and without competition, they all did well.

Support to businesses was based on loyalty and friendship. And customer service was always unbeatable. Courtesy was their main rule, and it worked better than any form of marketing. There was only one Ice cream shop— the children's paradise. Occasionally, Tom, the town's clown, showed up. I never knew if the business owners hired him or what his source of income was, but we saw him at the ice cream shop, the picnics, certain games, and sometimes even at school.

There were also two restaurants, very different from one another— one was casual, and that's where the young people gathered. It was the typical diner where they served hamburgers, hot dogs, milkshakes, pies, and all the popular American food. And the most appealing part was the jukebox—we always made sure to have at least a ten-cent coin for the jukebox to listen to our favorite song.

For the adults, there was a formal restaurant. Too fancy for my taste. That's where our parents liked to go— the Frenchman's restaurant, that's how everyone knew it. Only a few people knew the owner's name. They all called him the Frenchman, a widower with three daughters, and each had an assigned task at the restaurant. Their food didn't make me happy. I did not have to complicate my life with those unknown, sophisticated dishes. I was fine eating hamburgers and hot dogs, but I recall my parents and all their friends saying that if someone knew how to cook, it was the Frenchman. All the wealthy men with elevated status chose to take their families to a fancy restaurant on Sundays after church instead of spending the day in the sun, watching the neighbor's kids playing baseball at a picnic.

Inside the restaurant stood seven or eight tables total, covered in blue and white patterns, and when there were more customers than usual and all the tables were taken, the Frenchman sent two of his daughters to their house across the street for an extra table. They were always prepared with more chairs at the entrance, available for these cases.

Living in a safe and healthy environment, my life suffered a dramatic change at the beginning of the '60s decade.

SEVEN

Since my first day in college, I fell in love with Mikey, and the feelings were mutual. We studied together and did homework together. His parents bought him a motorcycle for his eighteenth birthday. It was the best present, not only for him but for me as well. I loved it when he picked me up on Saturdays to ride around, and we went to school parties, the movies, and many other places, but it wasn't until the end of the year that we decided to make our relationship official.

His parents and mine had a close friendship. The two families were like one, and when we started dating, everyone shared our happiness. We don't know who was happier, Mikey and me, or our families.

We used to make plans to go to the same university, hoping they would accept both of our applications at the same one. Since I was a little girl, I leaned toward a teaching career. I never doubted what I would do in life. Mikey was undecided between being a lawyer or a doctor. It was not until his second year of college that he knew medicine was his vocation, and due to his mother's hypothyroidism illness, he wanted to become an endocrinologist.

We could classify the decade we lived in as the derailment era— being a virgin after fourteen was a shame everyone wanted to hide, and at eighteen, exaggerating the frequency of sex seemed like an obligation for all. In the year 63, I was already in my first year of college. By then, things were dramatically different from the previous years. New British rock and roll bands such as the Beatles and the Rolling Stones spread rapidly in the USA. Women were crazy for them, and men followed their bell-bottom pants, vests, and long hairstyle trends. But that was only the soft part of that time.

Drugs, alcohol, and free sex overflowed, and all the youth, at least in this country, which I'm familiar with, wanted to behave according to the stream of customs. We started drinking. My friends and I indulged in whiskey sours because of the subtle taste and sophisticated name. They seemed harmless, and without noticing it, we ended up many times unable to walk. We also started to smoke cigarettes and soon moved on to marijuana. The adrenaline of making the marijuana joints was an unparalleled sensation. Not long after, LSD awakened our curiosity. We could say that we experienced everything. Mostly, it was due to the frenzy of wanting to live our youth at the same unstoppable pace as most young people.

There is something that leads me to believe now that I've lived most of my life, that what saved us at that time from hitting rock bottom and staying there as many others did were the values that our parents knew how to instill in us, or because we lived in a small city in which we followed the traditions of a healthy coexistence, and youth feared to fail their parents who always worked hard to give their children the best of examples, but, the truth is, we always knew how to make it on our own.

We could consider Mikey, Sandy, and me as moderate. If back then, moderation existed, but it's no secret, as the saying goes in Spanish, that Los principios no se ganan, se maman, which translates to *You don't win principles, you drink them*— through your mother's breastfeeding, you carry them before birth on her womb, you breathe them through the first contact with your father when he holds you in his arms. And birds of a feather flock together, the three of us were like branches of the same tree.

In our second year of college, Xavier, Sandy's boyfriend, joined our group. For Sandy, it was love at first sight. The attraction was mutual, and after a few weeks, they were together. But after Xavier joined the group, something changed. Sandy wanted to be with him all the time, the same way that Mikey and I were always together, and looking for those intimate moments alone, we anxiously waited for the Saturday outdoor movies.

The heat running through our veins with a slight skin touch was indescribable. We longed for our admittance to the university, sharing the same apartment and spending every night together, waking up in the morning one next to the other, enjoying our closeness from which no one could keep us apart.

Mikey was an attractive guy, six feet, one inch— athletic, a football player by hobby, and although it didn't fit his plans to become a professional player, he was always disciplined in his practices and games. He was kind and educated. Unspoken words emanated from his serene blue eyes and transported me each time we held each other's gaze, but his warm smile attracted me the most. He and Xavier spent hours discussing football, players, teams, coaches, or anything related.

Xavier was not as handsome as Mikey. However, his list of admirers was endless. It was not precisely his looks they felt attracted to, but his eloquence in speech, too much for my taste. He knew how to make any woman fall for him. He was more than friendly, a womanizer by nature. I didn't like him for Sandy, but every time I subtly touched the subject, she got upset, so I decided not to interfere, hoping my friend didn't end up disappointed and hurt.

The two couples used to hang out, enjoying our student times and planning the future. Since there was only one year left to finish college, we frequently based our conversations on the uncertainty of our admission to the university. If something I disapproved of was Xavier's extreme kindness addressing women, all of them, sometimes so noticeable, it felt offensive for Sandy. But perhaps my lack of approval was also due to Xavier's poor aspirations. While Mikey, Sandy, and I planned our future careers, Xavier was undecided. He intended to travel to Saint Lucia Island in the Caribbean, spend a few weeks there, and, if possible, work for a year at one of the tourist resorts.

One week before ending the semester before the last of college, we went to the end-of-the-school-semester ball. I had an unforgettable night with my boyfriend, not only because of the magical time we spent together but because after a few drinks, he was excessively loving and tender during the whole evening. He repeatedly told me how much he loved me, how fortunate he had been to find a girl like me, and that he couldn't understand what he did to deserve that much happiness. That night was incredible. I wished that it would never have ended. I wished it for other reasons than the ones destiny had in store for me after that enchanting evening.

Once they left Sandy and me at our homes, Xavier said he had forgotten his driver's license at the ball and asked Mikey to go back with him to pick it up, that it would be only for a moment. It might have been my imagination, but something fishy floated in the air. I noticed it in Xavier's attitude, who was a master at pushing Mikey into unwanted situations.

Seven more days of classes announced the proximity to summer break.

On a Monday, two weeks after coming back to classes, something strange was going on— whispers all over seemed to stop as I approached, and at times, I even felt like people pitied me. The atmosphere was heavy. I asked Sandy if she knew the reason, but she, like me, was not aware of anything.

At lunchtime, Mikey asked me to sit at an isolated table, the farthest away from all curious eyes but I still felt the burning looks coming from all directions. Suddenly, Mikey broke the silence.

"Please, I need to know that you're going to forgive me," he whispered without me knowing what he was guilty of or the reason for his repentance. "You know you are the only woman I want to spend the rest of my life with. I have loved you forever, and I've never been unfaithful. I'm telling you this because soon, you will learn about my mistake, and I prefer to be the one who tells you before you find out through someone else."

Invaded by an uneasy, nagging sensation, I continued without understanding what he was talking about. Startling anxiety was taking over me, and at the same time that I wanted to get to the bottom of that talk, I did not want to get to it either. Finally, avoiding eye contact, he spread the truth, burning every cell of my being— Melina, a girl known as the zipper for being in the pants of all the guys in college, was pregnant, and rumors were that he was the father. The night of the ball, when they went back, supposedly to take care of the license issue, Xavier already had a plan with Melina's girlfriend.

"You know," Mikey kept on repeating, "that I have never been unfaithful to you, but I had too much to drink that night. I don't even know how it happened. I don't recall a thing. All I know is that Xavier asked me how things went with Melina the day after." At that moment, I understood what he meant. And I felt shame, rage, and desperation. I never said anything to you because it was only one night when I made a mistake. I was ashamed and sure that it would never happen again."

My hands knotted atop my knees. My face paled. In an instant, I saw my world destroyed. Feeling anger and pain, humiliation ate me alive. Mikey begged me not to leave him, saying I was the love of his life and if the baby were his, he would take care of him responsibly— but he wanted nothing to do with Melina. He wished to continue our plans, and swore he would never make the same mistake again, but I couldn't be sure. Respect and trust had been lost, and no one could assure me that what he had done, he wouldn't do again, so I kept carrying my cross and my humiliation until the end of the school year. I focused on my studies and my university applications.

The semester felt eternal. But nothing is, and all deadlines are met. Finally, I was accepted at the University of Santa Barbara in California, as I wanted. Sandy was admitted to UCSD in La Jolla. We could not be together as we would have liked, but at least the two of us ended up in California. Any given long weekend, we arranged to spend it together, and during summer vacations, we saw each other again in our hometown when we reunited with our families.

EIGHT

Mariana

My life continued with moderate tranquility. Occasionally, the pain stored within me surfaced, pulling me toward a state of depression, but the moment I saw my Papa Jimmy all my fears disappeared. And all I wanted to do, was to enjoy his company while I could. His closeness gave me strength and helped me forget.

The relationship with my mother was far from perfect. I always disapproved of her behavior, and seeing her continuously searching for the ideal man despite having by her side the best man life could have given her made me feel something hard to explain. Primarily, was the fear of my Papa Jimmy leaving us one day and taking away from me all of that serenity and appreciation of life.

Frequently, my parents argued, always for the same reason. It hurt my dad, who was many years older than my mom, to see her wearing her best clothes and trying to look pretty when she left the house for several hours without saying where she was going. The relationships she occasionally had with other men lasted a short time, and the sheep always returned to the flock— but the wounds and fear intensified within me and my Papa Jimmy.

My dad's health was never good. He was the opposite of the ones following the rules to keep health in good shape. He had diabetes, high blood pressure, and high cholesterol. Although he always kept his sight in perfect condition, the same as his memory, he started to develop arthritis and heart problems, among others. He depended on a cabinet full of medications, having to pay the high bill that the desire to be healthy causes with side effects.

Coupled with all the complicated conditions of the human body were the emotional problems that my mom's behavior, without intention, caused him. His blood pressure started to soar, and looking for a way of escape provoked a stroke that left him paralyzed on one side of his body.

From then on, things changed drastically. The protection we always had by his side disappeared. Sometimes, I ask myself if we would've had the economic means to have found a reputable cardiologist or if we could've paid a therapist to help him recover his mobility, maybe things would have been different. But our scant income couldn't do the miracle. At first, my mom took him to the hospital. I was too young to remember if it was the General Hospital or the Social Security clinic. All I remember is how hard it was taking him to his therapies.

By then, he was overweight, and my mom and I, and when my grandma was at home, also helped us carry him, but it was hard for us, first to put him in the taxi and then to get him out, so the visits to the therapist and the doctor became less frequent each time.

We had him at home, and we all suffered— us by seeing him in such a state, and he, knowing that we saw him like that. I was eleven years old when this happened. I knew nothing about the latest advances in medicine, but I spent my days wishing for the miracle of one day seeing him recover and go back to the way he was before.

As time passed, my hope vanished, my child's fear gradually returned, and my apprehension of being unprotected grew. Slowly, the metamorphosis in my personality developed, and my joy for living left. Inside me, that internal fight, provoking, on the one hand, to let myself be carried away by the survival instinct and, on the other, to reach the end, was taking place. I distanced myself from my friends and started missing school, and the desire to learn new things seemed like a strange visitor in my short existence.

The area where we lived was unsafe. My Papa Jimmy, a few months before his stroke, gathered my mom and me— it was unclear if he had this foreboding about his future, or if his heart sent him signals that soon it would fail, or if protecting us above anything else became his priority but, he said that he had something important to tell us. He insisted, though, that it was a secret and we had to keep it as such.

At first, my mom disapproved of me being there and taking part in that conversation, but my dad convinced her. "Mariana is a smart girl," he said. "I could only have peace of mind knowing she has a way to defend herself when we're not around." That said, he extracted a gun from a red toolbox kept under the bed.

"You must never touch this gun." He continued with undefinable unease. "When the time comes, I will teach you how to use it, but always remember this— under any circumstance, you should get close to this box and use this firearm unless you find yourselves in extreme need to do so and only with the purpose of self-defense, in the meantime, I want you to forget that the gun is here and never come close to this box."

In the beginning, that talk made no sense to me, and neither did the reason for my Papa Jimmy to have a gun inside the house. In my mind, guns were only used in the movies. But as

I listened to the explanation, I realized the pistol was there as a preventive action, and the only time we should use it was in the rare but possible case of being assaulted or attacked. Then, things became clear.

"This area is too dangerous," my dad insisted. "Mariana is a gorgeous girl. Before we know it, her body will start changing. And it will be a temptation for any evil-minded man. If one day someone breaks into this house when I'm not here, I need to have the tranquility that you will be able to defend yourselves."

Among a series of instructions that my mom and I received, the main one was that when we detected someone forcing the door lock, or even worse, if the intruder was already inside, to shoot him without asking questions, just run and take the gun and shoot with no hesitation. He also said that we had to make sure to act rapidly before they did, because if they had a firearm, a knife, or something else that could harm us, then the danger would multiply.

If at that time, I felt scared at the beginning of the talk, in the end, I felt important, as I had not felt before. I thought I was not a child anymore. My Papa Jimmy saw me as a grown-up and could deposit all his trust in me. I wanted to tell my friends about it, and temptation burned me more each time, but the thought of betraying my dad's trust surpassed the desire to share the secret.

Trying to forget the whole thing, I focused on the security of knowing I had a gun to defend myself if I ever needed it. Occasionally, the nightmares of what I lived in my childhood visited me, and I wanted to have the reassurance of never again going through any man's sexual abuse, mainly from a much older man with dominance delusions only because he thinks that it is up to him to have control of the situation.

During several weeks and maybe even months, I felt fortunate each time I remembered the day my Papa Jimmy shared the news about the gun he so secretly kept and the day not long after when he taught us how to use it. That firearm had a purpose— but it never crossed my dad's mind that it could also be a double-edged sword.

My dad's care and attention routines became burdensome with time. However, that didn't affect me. It was the fear of seeing him going at such a fast pace. I didn't want nor could I imagine what my life would be like once he was gone. But we humans can't stop, not even prevent the inevitable, and, under those circumstances, I only focused on one thing— to go ahead of destiny and give it a blow before it hit me.

The idea of ending up alone with my mom again and being exposed to her mistreatments terrified me, for the most part, it was her constant search for her prince charming that she hadn't found up to then— and the thought of her bringing home another Eustolio or any other man wanting to abuse me because in my mind saturated with fear, I imagined that all men acted the same way, and this time, I would not allow it.

The thoughts rattled around my head, converged all the time at the same place— the red toolbox my Papa Jimmy jealously watched, and he confided it to us with an opposite purpose than the one that now my mind could not dispose of. Undoubtedly, there were other possibilities, but if we have the tool in our hands, ¿why look for a different alternative? That was the most viable, quick, uncomplicated, and perhaps the most accurate way to achieve the goal embedded in my mind, and that, for several days, I couldn't put away. But there was a sole obstacle— that my dad could not leave the house on his own. And I couldn't move him or take him anywhere by myself either.

If that reason stopped me for a few days, they weren't many. My desperation, my anguish, and the desire to put an end to everything that consumed me weighed more than anything else. At the age of twelve, we don't measure consequences. We only follow our impulses and do what we feel at a given moment that should be done without imagining what comes after. Based on that and wanting to get rid of thoughts that could stop my wrong intentions, I tried to control the shaking in my legs and, without hesitation, went straight to the cot, stretching my hand under to reach the red toolbox. Something told me not to turn back, but I could not avoid it. I turned and looked at my Papa Jimmy, motionless in his armchair. I wished I'd never seen it, but I saw the expression of horror on his face. Unfortunately, my decision was made. And I had no intention of going back.

NINE

"How handsome you look, son, with your new waiter uniform. We were lucky that they gave you the job at this new restaurant. I'm sure that in a few months, you will be able to save some money. Those rich people that eat there leave a bunch in tips."

"Yes, Dad. I think so. For now, I will try my best. Being the restaurant *the spot*, everybody wants to eat there, and that place receives dozens of applications. All the servers and bartenders would like to work there. I was lucky to be chosen, and I don't want to give them a reason to fire me."

"¿Did you hear that, son?"

"Yes, Dad, it sounded like a gunshot."

"Dear God! And it came from Jimmy's house. Susana is not at home. There's only him, the kid, and the grandmother. Come, run, let's see what happened."

"No. Wait, Dad. ¿What if there's a burglar inside with a gun?"

"No, son. No one is coming here willing to kill to steal only 100 pesos. The burglars know that there's no money in these houses. If they want to take the risk, they will do it at the fancy homes."

"Then, let's go."

"Good heavens! Ines, ¿who shot this poor creature?"

"She, herself. I was dozing while listening to my radio soap opera and heard the noise. I could see when the gun fell from her hand."

"Dad, is she dead?"

"No. But her pulse is weak, and she is losing too much blood. We need to take her to the hospital immediately."

"Dad, what if they blame one of us, thinking we were the ones who shot her?"

"No, son, there's no time now to think about that. Don't you see that the girl is too young to let her die?"

"You're right, Dad. I'll get the car, and we'll take her to the hospital."

"Not you. You only start the car, as it takes a while to get warm. Tell your mom to come and stay with Ines taking care of Jimmy, and tell your brother, Ruben, to come with me to help me. In the meantime, you get going to work. You will have to ride the bus this time."

"Please, Don Armando, save my granddaughter. I beg you. Don't let her die."

"With the help of the Virgin Guadalupe, everything will be fine, Ines. But please, quickly, bring an old shirt from Jimmy to put on Mariana's wound. We need to press hard to prevent her from bleeding to death."

"Ruben, help me, hurry up! We must put her in the car. Extremely carefully! You go in the back seat with her, pressing the wound until we arrive at the hospital."

"Dad, what if the car leaves us somewhere? You know it is always failing."

"Let's hope that won't happen now. Our little car sometimes acts whimsical, but it always takes us and brings us back whenever we need it."

"Which hospital are we taking her to?"

"For now, let's go to the town's hospital. At least there's a doctor there. They will know what to do or where they will send her. Let's pray the Divine Providence won't allow this girl to die on the way."

"We have someone with a bullet wound, Doctor." One of the nurses said. "It's a girl. In a moment, we'll let the police know."

"Before that, call the chemist immediately. We need to analyze the blood, and once we have the results, let's ask for reinforcement at the blood banks in Tijuana and Ensenada. Hopefully, they won't have the blood shortage we constantly experience here."

"The gentleman that comes with the girl is her neighbor. He says he can locate the mother."

"Go and tell him to reach her urgently, but first, call Tijuana and ask them to send an ambulance for the patient. From what I see, the bullet is dangerously close to the heart. It probably went through her ribs, and I don't know if there's damage to the lung. We need to operate immediately. But we don't have adequate equipment here. Please make sure the ambulance gets here as soon as possible. It's a matter of life and death."

"Right away, Doctor. We'll tell them to be prepared in Tijuana when the girl arrives."

"Also, verify if they have a surgeon on premises and, once we know the patient's blood type, while the ambulance gets here, send a press bulletin to the radio requesting blood donors. Include the broadcasters of Tijuana and Ensenada as well."

"Come, son, while the ambulance arrives, let's bring Susana. You heard the doctor. They want a close relative to sign the papers. The police won't take long to start investigating the case. It is best if the mother is aware of what's happening."

"And if she decided to be at a different zone today, ¿how are we finding her? We never know where she's going to be."

"I think I know where she is. Lately, she's been doing well outside that elementary school. Most likely, that's where she will be."

"The good thing is that it's not rush hour. If it was, we could not even get close to the school."

"I'll push the accelerator and be there in less than three minutes."

"I saw the candy cart, Dad. There she is!"

"I can't get that close driving. You get out of the car, run, and explain to Susana what happened. Tell her you will watch over her cart. And ask her to accompany me to the hospital. I will come later to pick you up."

"Are you the mother of the wounded girl?"

"Yes, but you don't seem to work in the hospital. Who are you?"

Flashing their badges, the two men identified themselves as policemen. "We need to ask you some questions."

"If you, please excuse me, gentlemen," the doctor interrupted— "the ambulance is arriving, we must transfer the patient immediately. If you like, you can follow them, and once you get there, you can work on your investigation. There's no time to waste, and it is helpful if the mother is with the patient in the ambulance. You can activate your siren if you wish."

= = = = =

I lost the notion of time between my transfer and the surgery. When I left the operating room, I was a living dead. My mother, in the meantime, tried to talk to the doctor while being interrogated by the judicial police.

When the doctor came out of the operating room, my mom, who had been waiting for several hours, approached him.

"Where is my daughter, doctor? Is she dead?"

"No, Ma'am. Your daughter is alive. It was a complicated surgery to extract the bullet, but we achieved it. Unfortunately, the girl is delicate. It is necessary to keep her under observation and optimal care until she comes out of that state."

"What state? Can I see her?"

"Only for a moment, but I must warn you— she won't be able to talk to you. She is in a coma."

"What does that mean?"

"A coma is a state which makes the body incapable of expressing or reacting to emotions. It doesn't have movement, either. Most likely, it is a vegetative state until the inflammation of the brain, which in most cases is the cause of a coma, subsides. You can see your daughter for a moment if you wish."

"Doctor, it looks like she's dead. Could you please come and see her?"

"Don't be scared. Your daughter is not dead. That is the state she's going through, but she is still alive."

"If they extracted the bullet, why did she end up like this?"

"I couldn't tell you for sure. It is possible that when she received the bullet impact, she suddenly collapsed, and a sharp fall may have caused such a severe brain inflammation that provoked a coma."

"How long is she going to be like this?"

"I wish I would have that answer, but unfortunately, that's something I couldn't tell you either. They might be days, perhaps weeks. From what I understand, she tried to commit suicide. Sometimes, the desire to live and the stimulation the patients receive from the people around them help. The important thing here is that every time you talk to her, do it about positive things to induce motivation."

"And if I do that, do you think my daughter will be all right?"

"Under these circumstances, the intervention of a social worker will help. Also, psychological therapy will be needed. Suicide attempt cases are tough. Sadly, they are more frequent than we would think, above all, among youngsters. For now, it is imperative to count on a good psychologist and a social worker."

"But then, while my daughter is still alive. Is she going to live like dead? We already have my partner at home with a stroke. And if he's there, unable to move, and my daughter is here, and she can't move either, then what do I do? I need to go to work, and we live in Tecate."

"Would've you preferred she had died?"

"No. Of course not. Don't say that, Doctor. I'm grateful to Virgin Guadalupe for keeping my daughter alive. What I meant is that I must work. And I can't take care of both at the same time."

"Once the investigators decide you can leave, you can return to Tecate. Your daughter will be transferred to another hospital where doctors and nurses will take care of her, and you can stop by to see her to the best of your ability and to see if she is progressing. If she wakes up, they will contact you by phone."

"But we don't have a phone in the house."

"Don't worry. You can leave your mobile phone number."

"Cell. Phone? That's for rich people, although I have seen some merchants in my zone who have them. However, for me, that's out of the question. Since my partner is sick at home, I hardly make enough to buy food."

"Do you have the contact of a neighbor where they can locate you?"

"At the grocery store *The Little One,* two blocks from my house, I often go there to make phone calls, and when somebody needs to locate me, they leave me a message. If it's urgent, the kid from the owner goes to my house to let me know."

"Then, stay calm. I need to deliver the last instructions for your daughter's transfer. Someone will contact you to inform you which hospital she will be in."

"You heard the doctor, Susana. Here's some water. Or, if you prefer, my kid can get you a glass of horchata or agua fresca."

"Thank you, Don Armando. I don't know what would have happened to Mariana hadn't you been there. God only knows what got into her head to do such a thing."

"These days, young people think differently than we used to when we were young. It seems as if they don't adapt or belong anywhere. Besides, Mariana always wears a sad look. Perhaps seeing Jimmy in such a condition has affected her deeply. But also, she might carry other things inside that dragged her to this situation."

"That child has suffered since she was a little girl. She's never happy with anything, and me, being so busy with my things— because I never had it easy either, I haven't been able to pay full attention to her."

"It's never too late, Susana, to amend our mistakes. With the help of God and the Virgin Guadalupe, you'll see how things change. Mariana is still young. Maybe you can advise her to start looking at things differently. I don't know much about the young ones trying to commit suicide, but I think it's best not to reprimand her and give her all the help she needs. It's important to let her know she's not alone. And the rest will come with time."

TEN

For several weeks, I lost the notion of time, but what is time if not a personal perception? For someone whose life is in danger, one minute of waiting for help might seem like an eternity. For us who learned to breathe at birth, thirty seconds underwater feels like an hour. For an athlete giving his best effort to reach the goal before his competitors, one second late could represent years of frustration— and on the other side of the coin, for a family that has only a week's vacation to enjoy it among the loved ones, seven days turn into one and for a couple in love that will have to separate after a weekend, this might feel like an instant.

    Submerged in my abyss of darkness, I didn't feel or think. I didn't experience pain. Time passed by, taking me with it. Succumbing to that maze of unnoticed immensity, after two weeks, my flight initiated its landing. I softly started to come down until I touched the earth. It was perhaps a slight movement of my fingers or one tear appearing at the corner of my eye— my state of unconsciousness didn't allow me to witness the awakening. All I remember is being in a hospital room, connected to several tubes and monitors, which now, I understand, had the purpose of keeping me alive when I was incapable of this function despite my intentions being the opposite.

The silence and quietness of my loneliness switched to the commotion originated by my slight movement the minute it was detected by the nurse, who was the first one to notice the change in me. Hasty steps circulated through my room. Excited yet soft voices of a couple of doctors and nurses surrounded my bed. As I regained consciousness, I didn't know if all or most of the hospital staff approached my room as those who attended a circus wanting to be on the first row not to miss a single show detail.

There was one doctor who seemed to be instructing the first team. Frequently, unfamiliar faces of doctors, nurses, and other hospital personnel, even medical students, showed up. After twenty-four hours, they could finally reach my mom, and with her, the second group appeared. Besides the hospital staff, a social worker, one priest, and two gentlemen, whom I knew later, were part of the investigation bureau of the judicial police.

In the middle of all this chaos, I was still there, breathing, remembering, and suffering. I did not understand what went wrong with my plan. Before shooting myself, I recalled placing the gun in my chest. It was supposed to be an instantaneous death. At what point did the bullet deflect and pierce between my ribs? I guess that is the result of a young rookie trying to execute an action that, as absurd as it sounds, requires practice to achieve perfection, as most things in life do.

It is hard to identify what was more excruciating— the physical and psychological recovery activities with all those therapies and procedures required in this case or the constant interrogation by the police who, although they knew they were dealing with a suicidal attempt, focused on discharging the possibility of a second person involved or a person of interest in all this theatrical act.

The visits of the investigating agents were more frequent than any convalescent patient could resist— at the most unexpected moments, and, when more than anything else, I needed to rest, I had to deal with these two dark-haired and mustache men, one of them shorter and the other one stocky, always wearing dark glasses and a brown leather jacket. This last one seemed to be leading the investigation. They repeatedly asked the same questions. They questioned me first and then my mom. And afterward, both of us. As if there were not enough criminals loose in the streets that should be interrogated, these two men focused on my case with such tenacity that now that I think about it, they could've made me feel important.

I woke up every morning in my struggle to face one more day, and as soon as the nurses left, the inquisition phase took place.

Where did I get the gun? How long ago did I have it? Who taught me how to use it? Where did I hide it? Who was with me at the time of the shot? Was there someone else pushing me toward that decision? And a series of questions leading us nowhere after being repeated so many times. There was no end to the interrogating process. However, to my and my mom's surprise, one day, those two gentlemen said goodbye, and we didn't see them again. At least that was one less bean in the burlap sack.

When they left, my tiredness diminished, and I could concentrate on my recovery, not that I was anxious to recover as the doubts were still present in my mind— did I want to recover, knowing that meant to continue living and that was not within my plans? Or perhaps I was grateful for the second chance life gave me? That's what everyone at the hospital tried to convince me of. But I believe that was mostly about my desire to leave that place.

The weariness of taking all that medication, the physical

therapies, and the evident pity I caused everyone around me drove me to want to go back home as soon as possible. The entire hospital, including the staff and the patients were aware of my situation, and, on the other hand, the newspapers that dedicated their first page to my story contributed to spreading the gossip through the whole city of Tecate, which more likely fell in the category of a village where nothing out of the ordinary ever happens, and this was undoubtedly the happening of the century.

One day when I was in the *'escolar'* which is how they called the children's recovery section, one unknown girl approached me— she was thirteen years old, with multiple fractures on her clavicle, humerus, radius, and ulna of her left arm.

"You're the one who tried to commit suicide, right?" She asked me as she moved slowly toward me with the help of a wheelchair maneuvered with her right hand only. With a mix of annoyance and discomfort, I slightly turned my face in her direction, thinking it was none of her business what I did or didn't do.

"I would like to speak with you," she said in such a soft voice that forced me to try hard to understand her. "Where did you get the courage?" She asked, and then, she added— "I want to do the same. My parents and my little brother just died in a car accident. They said my dad fell asleep while driving, the car overturned, and I was the only one who got out alive, but now that I'm alone, I don't want to continue living. I have an aunt who has been calling. I don't know her. She doesn't live here. But I don't need an aunt. What I need are my parents and my little brother. I want to die, but I don't know how. I'm scared. I'm catholic, so were my parents and they taught me that we're not supposed to end our lives. It is God who decides when our time arrives."

On that day, after spending two weeks in the hospital in a state of coma, for the first time, I saw things through a different mirror. I thought about the pain of that young girl, who, according to her conversation, had a good relationship with her family and, now she had lost them, all of them at the same time, remaining alone in this world and, with her fractures, she might not even be able to practice any sport or dance or do some other activities. She would have limitations in the future. Every loss entails sadness, but this unfortunate girl, besides her physical pain, her loneliness prevented her from being happy to be alive.

At that moment, the same recurrent thought since I started recovering my consciousness came back to my mind— *my Papa Jimmy*. I remembered the look of horror on his face, although I only saw him for an instant before my suicide attempt. Ashamed, I tried not to make eye contact, but I couldn't avoid turning and seeing him even for a second, for I needed to see him for the last time. But now that I was still alive and with my classmates' visits and the affection everyone strove to express to me, my perception of life was changing, and my desire to leave the hospital to be able to hug my dad and tell him how sorry I felt to have caused him that pain, was eating me alive.

A few days before my release, the girl with the fractured bones revisited me. But this time with a different attitude.

"I came to say goodbye," she said, "and to tell you that when God shuts a door, he always opens a window. I'm moving to Chihuahua with my aunt. She's my dad's sister. She and her husband have three boys— one is seven, the other is five, and the baby is one year old. My aunt says they always wanted a girl. And now they want to adopt me. They own a bakery in Chihuahua where they also make chocolates, and if I want to, they can teach me how to make them, and I like that idea. They also talked about the high school I'm going to attend. And they showed me pictures of their house. I haven't been to Chihuahua. I didn't imagine that one day I would live there, but you know what? I like the idea of having a family again.

Loneliness terrified me, but now, I won't be alone, and my parents, wherever they are, will continue watching over me."

As this girl, whose depression previously seemed stronger than mine, left the room, I realized that her fate had reverted, and that brought me a breath of hope. Perhaps not everything in life was as negative as I thought. The circumstances may change as well as our future. Although I felt distant from experiencing happiness, from feeling safe again as the first day that I learned to ride a bike, now I caressed a different emotion, knowing that someone waited for me at home— my Papa Jimmy not only awaited my return, but he also needed me and feeling needed, knowing that I could be helpful to anyone, gave me hope.

Accelerating my recovery efforts after nine days of the encounter and the talk with that girl, I managed to leave the hospital. My memory, the same as my body, was still weak. Above all, it was hard for me to focus and remember exactly what happened, but the thought of seeing my dad again provoked my enthusiasm. On his condition, I did not know how much time he had left. I saw him getting weaker each time on the last days I spent at home. Suddenly, an obscure thought, followed by a chilling sensation, took over me. *What if my Papa Jimmy passed while I was in the hospital, and my mom didn't tell me to avoid adding more days of depression to my calendar?*

ELEVEN

Upon discharge from the hospital, I could perceive a change in my life and realized that things wouldn't be as easy as I thought. We had to ride the bus back home. My mother and I were used to this way of transportation, except that in my condition, it was exhausting as the bus didn't go up as far as where we lived. Because of our precarious situation, we couldn't afford the luxury of taking a taxi. It was a steep hill, and I was still weak, too weak. I tried my best to lean on my mom, and she made a significant effort to help me, but my weakness and weariness didn't allow us to advance quickly.

    The long road seemed to be steeper every time. Reaching home felt like an eternity. I was impatient to feel the closeness of that home, and although humble, my rush to arrive grew with each step. In my mind, I had a vivid image of my Papa Jimmy—the expression on his face when I shot myself, my desperation to get home and ask for his forgiveness, my fear of finding him more deteriorated than the last time I saw him, the uncertainty of not knowing if he wanted to see me again and if he had missed me as much I missed him and the affliction of guilt, knotted in my brain and squeezed so hard, causing a sharp pain.

After the endless stretch by foot that took us longer than the bus ride from the hospital, we finally approached the little blue house. The pounding in my heart felt like it was about to explode.

On my first step inside the house, my sight was directed to Papa Jimmy's armchair, and I threw myself into his arms. Crying, I asked for his forgiveness. He couldn't hug me, but my hug was worth the hugs for the both of us. I didn't want to let go of him, and I could see the spring of tenderness in his sight. I knew he had forgiven me before I asked him to.

I don't know how much time I spent sitting next to him, relishing the reality of his presence. I never wanted to leave his side. I thanked God for allowing me to continue living. And for giving me that precious opportunity of reconciliation with my dad and to show him my repentance for causing him all that grief, knowing he was in that condition.

Having settled my past debts, I continued with my therapies and my hospital visits, where they consistently took x-rays of my chest to make sure there was no severe damage in my lung since the gunshot entered less than one inch below my left breast with a shocking proximity to the heart, piercing not only my chest but also part of my lung.

My first memories after waking up from the coma in the hospital were about how hard it was for me to focus. I felt like waking up from a deep sleep, so heavy that all I thought about was going back to sleep. My weakness was superior to my will. All I did was follow orders from the doctors and nurses.

Over time, I started to remember what, in the beginning, lodged in darkness in my memory. I thought about the unbearable pain in my chest, which grew every time with each breath or my effort to breathe.

I also recollected the investigators when they asked my mom why she wasn't crying during my transfer to the hospital, to which she answered that each of us has a different way of showing our emotions and that she didn't have to cry like a runaway goat.

At first, the therapies exhausted me, and not having the means of comfortable transportation tired me right from the get-go— but we adapt to everything in this life. And those of us who have never had commodities and lack everything easily adjust to inconveniences. And under those circumstances, I progressed in my task of being the way I was before.

As I slowly recovered my memory, I regained my strength and security when walking and making some movements. Getting on and off the bus became lighter. Although it was still hard, I didn't feel the torture of the first time. My therapies were working, and my recovery continued following its course until the day came when I could go back to school.

All my classmates treated me with kindness. I will never know if they did it out of pity, or because I was considered a celebrity after my story appeared on the first page of the local newspapers, or because they were grateful to me for bringing a town of not more than 55,000 inhabitants, on which rarely something interesting happened, a topic that gave them for weeks or months something to talk about, not only among adults but in all the children and classmates that knew me.

This kind of popularity overwhelmed me, but on the other hand, I started making new friends. I continued seeing my friend Karina, but not for long, since her father was transferred to the state of Sonora, and the whole family had to move— her father before the end of the school year, and Karina and her mom as soon as school was over and the Summer vacation started.

Besides Karina, there were four of us in our group, and we were together all the time. We used to go to the park, the movies, or the parties. And to did our homework together, even though this last activity was less frequent among my friends, except for Rosita, because that study thing didn't come easily to them.

DOMINANCE DELUSIONS

Among our group, each of us was characterized by a unique and very defined personality. At the same time, we were different from each other, and except for Karina, something kept the other four of us united— we felt identified as if we were players of the same team. We always tried to stay together, at least during the first years of our friendship. Little did we know about the direction we would follow in the future because the future was the last of our concerns.

That way, we continued the last year of elementary school and the period in which we all are still children with the same rush to be able to skip that phase, which dictates not only a different stage in our studies but, because being in high school, most of us become teenagers and, we experience significant changes in our bodies and our lives.

As I watched the time pass by, the days seemed endless. Pretty soon, we would enter that phase we were all waiting for— inseparable and impatient, without knowing that by remaining together throughout that bond that was already created, we would also continue together on the same destructive path impossible to prevent and from which Karina had the fortune to escape at the right time.

TWELVE

Being in high school was a beyond-belief experience. I liked learning science and anatomy. Studying the human body and knowing what's inside was fascinating. It attracted me to learn an array of new things, and at the same time, getting good grades gave me a sense of well-being but that was only the academic side, on which I focused the first year and part of the second. In the end, mainly in the third year, things began to take a different path, and the social aspect predominated.

What my group of friends and I caused made me feel good. The three of them possessed extraordinary physical beauty. I never considered myself to be at the same level as the rest. However, I was never at a disadvantage, either. At least, that's what everyone said. We stood out for our popularity. The boys at school followed us all the time. And to achieve a date with any of us was like getting a trophy that any guy wanted to show off.

One day, Selena, Malú, and I were walking toward the park when some guys riding a white Cadillac offered us a ride. Among them was Selena's brother's friend. Impressed by the luxurious new Cadillac right away, we said yes. It was a fun night. They stopped at a small grocery store and bought beer. That night, without fear, I crossed the line separating soft drinks from alcoholic beverages.

At first, I thought the taste of beer was not my thing. I found it hard to understand how such a bitter drink could be so popular. But everyone drank it as if it had a pleasant flavor, and I didn't want to be left behind, so I forced myself to drink a couple that turned my stomach. Nevertheless, I didn't want to make it obvious, especially to Carlos Alberto, one of the guys in the group who seemed to drink like a bottomless barrel— while I counted his drinks, he tried to convince me that everything was a matter of getting used to and if I committed, soon I would be drinking at everyone else's pace.

I felt attracted to him, although we did not have time to talk in private, as that evening, we were part of the group, and we had no chance to get to know each other, but when the moment came to say goodbye, he asked me to go on a date with him the day after. Though I was dying to accept, I had to explain my situation to him, crossing my fingers so that it wouldn't be the last time he asked me out.

My mom asked me to go the morning after to the house, which they paid her to clean and take care of. That day, she could not fulfill her obligation since it was a long weekend in the U.S. and one of the best days to sell candy at the border crossing.

"Having the responsibility to be in that house doesn't mean we couldn't see each other." Carlos Alberto said, on the previous night, when he invited me to go out.

My heart pounded fast, realizing that perhaps he had the same feelings for me. "But, at what time could we meet?" I replied. "I must be there all day until my mom arrives at 11 p.m.."

"I can be there when you tell me. I can keep you company.

That way, you won't be alone, and I assure you, time goes much faster that way."

Interestingly, I noticed we were on the same page. I liked Carlos Alberto. And I was thrilled with the idea of spending several hours or perhaps most of the following day with him. I still didn't know much about him except that he had applied for a job at the Navy in San Diego, and apparently, he had passed the first interview. That attracted me even more.

The morning after, I entered the house at eleven o'clock, and by 2 p.m., Carlos Alberto arrived. We'd agreed on that time, although the three hours before his arrival seemed eternal. He showed up with carne asada tacos for the two of us. I frequently had them before, but I hadn't realized how delicious they were— this time, the tacos were no different from the others. It was the company that made a difference.

Besides the tacos, he brought beer. He drank four and I two. Surprisingly, now they were not bitter. This time, I enjoyed them. And I knew that soon, I would get into the habit of not only drinking beer but anything coming from Carlos Alberto or anything else he suggested.

We chatted for a whole day that seemed to pass by in a fleeting instant, and he talked to me about his family, especially his mother, with whom he lived, about his plans of working for the Navy and later moving to San Diego since he was a US citizen. He also brought up the topic everyone felt intrigued by— the matter of the suicide attempt. And if I felt uncomfortable before talking about it, I was glad to have a conversation topic that day. In my life, nothing interesting to talk about happened. That saved me from boring him or spending a day he wouldn't have wanted to repeat.

I didn't know if the owner of the house where we were was a hunting enthusiast, but he had a rifle on display in an unlocked glass case. What prompted me to open the glass case and extract the shotgun? I don't know either, but trying to make myself funny, I aimed it at Carlos Alberto.

"Leave that alone," he said with authoritarian demand. His words denoted anxiety. "Weapons are not to play, and above all, if you're not sure they are not loaded, never aim it at anyone."

By the expression on his face, I knew that he didn't find my joke funny. I opted to obey him and put the rifle back in its place. From our first time alone, I remember every detail, what each of us said, and how we both reacted, especially how he did to that incident. For a moment, I thought he wouldn't want to see me again, but in the end, my worries were dispelled, and the two of us decided to forget about my silly behavior.

From then on, Carlos Alberto and I saw each other often, and later, it was almost every day until the day they called him from the Navy. He moved to San Diego to start his training. I feared that would distance us, but on the contrary— On his days off, despite his exhaustion, he wanted to spend them with me. I was at the beginning of his list, and his time to relax occupied the last place.

By then, he was my boyfriend. My three friends also had boyfriends. The four couples got together on weekends, and the beer-drinking habit increased. We later introduced wine coolers to our preferences. The girls and I liked that tangy flavor, which we consumed more each time until it became addictive, and soon after, we discovered we wanted to try something different. We were curious about tequila. The taste was surprisingly sharper, but it didn't take me long to get used to it.

My relationship with my mom had improved since I left the hospital. But now, it had worsened. Although to her, drinking was okay, she disapproved every time I got home with an alcoholic breath. She argued that at my age, girls shouldn't start drinking, and the arguments became more frequent. The rejection toward my boyfriend and my friends increased.

I tried to ignore what my mom approved or disapproved of. I felt I found happiness next to Carlos Alberto, who wrapped me with his tenderness and attention. Life was showing me the unknown side that, in my first years, I didn't know existed.

At fourteen years old, I was different from most girls my age whose incessant anxiety leads them to the same path— to reach their fifteenth birthday and have a lavish quinceañera celebration with one spectacular cake, an expensive dress, an endless list of guests, being the birthday girl the center of attention, while her parents incur in lofty-debts of money to celebrate that stage on which a girl subtly crosses the line in life that leaves her childhood behind. Girls await, impatiently, the waltz moment to have the closeness with the guy they dream about, even awake.

There was a difference between adolescents next to becoming quinceañeras and me because, in my case, I had passed that cautious closeness to get to the bottom of intimacy with the guy of my dreams. And that made me feel good, given my childhood circumstances. Now, I had experienced being drained of desire next to the man I chose. Not as an animal-forced-act provoking since the beginning immeasurable repugnance, and along with it fear, not wanting to be alive, hate and rejection of life, and thinking that the value of a woman who can't be respected nor awake any consideration, reduces to its infamous expression.

Life was in debt to me, and wanting to make it up to me showed me the other side of the coin with Carlos Alberto, allowing me to live those moments of intimacy that start slowly to increase intensely out of control until we feel we're entering paradise, and give us a reason to wake up every morning with a smile in our lips with the immense desire that hours become instants to be able to be again with the person we love.

My days passed and I had only one thing on my mind— to spend as much time as possible with Carlos Alberto or talk to him constantly while he was in San Diego. Before initiating his training, he bought me a prepaid card for my cell phone, and each time he was away, he made sure to recharge the card so I would always be reachable when he had breaks and wanted to talk to me.

My graduation was close, but of all those initial plans and projects and my desire to learn more each time to finish triumphant, appearing with the highest grades among the first places slipped to the back burner. I didn't have enough time, or perhaps I didn't make time to pursue my goal, for achieving it meant spending less time with Carlos Alberto, talking less to him, or removing him briefly from my mind.

THIRTEEN

Katya

My period of adaptation at the university was reduced to three weeks. Afterward, I felt in my element. For the first time, I was studying at a place where I didn't see or talk to Sandy on every break. That was the hard part for the two of us. But since the beginning, we found a way to shorten the distance through phone calls at the end of the day to catch up with each other regarding the campus, the dorms, the classes, the most attractive teachers, and even the annoying ones, as well as the discoveries of classmates or students from other groups that we found interesting.

We relished being at the university, and even though it would've made us happy had we been accepted into the same one, we still felt closer than ever. On the first long weekend, I wanted to go to La Jolla. Sandy talked fondly about her university and the beaches of this enchanting city, and she was not the only one in love with La Jolla. Any person who had been there pushed me to plan a visit at the first opportunity.

Sandy had a large group of friends. And it made me happy to

see that she was adapting so fast. After breaking up with Xavier a few months before, she wanted to let time pass before getting involved in a serious relationship. Although she suffered at the beginning for a few weeks, and I felt sad to see her in such a state, I was happy when she decided to leave Xavier. She deserved better— someone faithful, who respected her, and whom she could trust and see as a loyal companion.

Upon my arrival to La Jolla, Sandy had a full itinerary since Friday evening. I could hardly drop off my suitcase when we were ready to start the party. The three days flew by. We wanted to do so much that, in the end, what was supposed to be a relaxed weekend would've ended up being strenuous for anyone. But not for Sandy or me. We spent most of the day at the beach. Arriving at the condominium, we showered and were ready for dinner at a good restaurant. Since a young age, I felt attracted to dining at fancy places, and Sandy, being such a good companion, was willing to eat anything I felt like. In the evenings, we went to parties with her friends, and on Sunday, we visited the San Diego Zoo, which was the first thing we had planned since we spoke about my trip to La Jolla. My love for animals forced me to tour a zoo in any city I visited.

On my return to Santa Barbara, the reality of being away from Sandy hit me, but I adapted focusing on my studies and activities. I joined a fraternity and appreciated aspects of life that were meaningless to me before. I also learned about the sisterhood developed with other students. On weekends, I worked for a pet store.

On the following long weekend, it was Sandy's turn to visit me in Santa Barbara, and our agenda, as busy as my trip to La Jolla, didn't allow us a moment of relaxation. We kept that closeness during the whole time of our studies. During our first two years, we took turns seeing each other in any of the two places we were studying. We always spent Christmas at home in Missouri, and before returning to our universities, we traveled with our families to Herman, where Sandy's grandparents owned a winery.

One of the most beautiful memories of my childhood was those getaways to the Herman wineries, where infinite peace and tranquility breathed, contemplating the insuperable sight of the vineyards from the house of the grandparents, as we all used to call them— a seven-bedroom English-style house, built at the beginning of the XX Century.

In the first two summers of our careers, we vacationed in Missouri in a family atmosphere. We indulged in the lakes, parks, and the quietness they were famous for. We loved being together and with our families. In the third year, the family activities stopped being as appealing as before. We wanted to use the wings of our freedom to fly farther away and explore new horizons.

Sandy spent the summer with a male friend in Newport Beach and I went to a girlfriend's house in San Francisco. Once I saw everything this lovely place offered, we went for a few days to Sonoma, where other classmates joined us.

Sandy and I had an extensive circle of friends. Occasionally, some became more than friends, but none of us was involved in a serious relationship.

Six months before the end of my studies, I realized that as a teacher, regardless of the state or teaching institution where I wanted to work, there would always be a considerable number of Latin students, and my Spanish was reduced to a dot above the basic level. After consulting with Sandy, we both agreed to spend a summer in Guadalajara to learn Spanish before starting to look for job options and send resumes.

This city had a reputation in the summertime of becoming one more U.S. city due to the immense number of North Americans going there to learn Spanish. Neither Sandy nor I had been to Mexico. The two of us were amazed by that experience which would mark the transition from students to professionals without knowing which direction we would take once established in our jobs. We were aware that life would pull us in different directions, and although the friendship of a lifetime never ends, the responsibilities create a great distance with time.

We didn't lose any sleep over separating at the end of the summer— we were determined to make the most of our trip, learning the Spanish language as much as possible and, at the same time, taking advantage of our stay, combining 20% of cultural activities with 80% of the fun. By dedicating that time to the cultural activities, we were more than generous since most of the young people who go through the Guadalajara experience, the part of learning about local traditions ends up buried in a place almost impossible to rescue.

It would've been unforgivable not to peek at the surface of the refined environment of Guadalajara. This impressive city overflows with art and culture on each of its corners. It has an astonishing variety of museums, historical monuments, theaters, and countless other attractions. We would've regretted not taking advantage of everything this beautiful place offers.

The first thing we discovered, and allow me to emphasize the first because this happened almost at the airport, even before we settled at the boarding house, was the Mexican guys practically hunting North American students. In the summer, numerous guys break their relationships with their girlfriends. Or the girls decide to break them because they can't stand the situation. At first, neither Sandy nor I understood the cause nor the euphoria for us foreigners. But soon, we realized that Guadalajara at that time was a strict, conservative city in which the girls, most of them used to daily mass, came from catholic families with the conviction of arriving at the altar being virgins on the day of their matrimony. Under those circumstances, the guys took the opportunity to enjoy an open-minded relationship and also open to many other things that they could not experience with the señoritas from Jalisco.

The customs were different. At the end of classes, the invitations to lunch or dinner were never lacking. And on weekends also to breakfast. We loved feeling so popular, but the most astounding was the serenades, part of a tradition, not only unknown to us but inconceivable coming from a country where respect surpasses many old habits and noise after 10 p.m. and disturbing the neighbors is illegal. In Guadalajara, there were serenades every weekend at any time after midnight.

The boarding house where we lived temporarily lodged eight foreign girls— two Swiss and six North American. And the serenades were a must on the weekends. If not for one of us it would be for the other. It excited us that they would wake us up any time after midnight with music. After one hour, the trio, mariachi, marimba, or whatever was hired, left, and the guys occasionally stayed talking with us through the window. And, when the guys and the musical group left, we stayed chatting until dawn.

If the imprudent actions of youth blind us, through time, we realize our injustices caused by the lack of maturity and without malice. The value of eight hours of sleep is not a secret. Now, I understand how difficult it must have been for the owners of boarding houses to tolerate this situation every weekend of summer due to the need for extra income, providing accommodation to students.

The serenades were not the only thing we liked about Guadalajara. Summertime was the rainy season. On occasions, the rain was so powerful that it seemed like it wanted to bring the roof down. The showers were always accompanied by lightning and thunder so loud as though the earth couldn't resist them. In the beginning, it scared us, but soon we got used to it. They only lasted a few minutes, and afterward, they left a trace of petrichor, the earthy scent produced by rain that, up to now, remained embedded in my memory, associated with good times.

DOMINANCE DELUSIONS

Apart from going to the theaters when we felt attracted to a play or concert, we were delighted to go to Casa de las Artesanías— House of Crafts. The richness of creativity from the entire country concentrated in this place impresses the most demanding customers. We viewed it as a shopping paradise, starting with blouses, shawls, purses, and jewelry. The color and the magic of these upscale art pieces win the heart of any buyer. Besides, the prices were ridiculously affordable. It almost made us uncomfortable to know that our money didn't pay for the time the artisans invested in these valuable artistic creations.

We also liked going shopping at the market, and the shopping method there was different— the embroidery, silver, ceramic, clay, and many others, without taking away their merit, didn't reach the quality of Casa de las Artesanías. At the market, it was customary, and the vendors expected the shoppers to bargain. To us, that was different and fun. After spending the day at the market, we directed ourselves toward Plaza del Mariachi, where we learned to drink tequila. By the time we visited the town of Tequila on the outskirts of Guadalajara, fascinating in every aspect, teaching us the origins and production of this internationally renowned alcoholic beverage product of the agave azul, we were already experts on this drink.

On the last day of our stay in Guadalajara, invited by some friends, we ate at El Abajeño restaurant, where we had a mariachi band playing at our table the whole afternoon. Afterward, our friends dropped us at El Tapatío Hotel near the airport. Previously, we'd arranged to spend our last night there since our plane would leave early the following morning.

Before retiring to our room, we took a peek at the bar to appreciate the spectacular view of the city. We sat for a minute, undecided if we wanted coffee, tea, or water. Tequila, we'd had enough during the afternoon.

"Do you mind if I join you?" Said someone who, despite being Mexican, his aspect was most likely Lebanese. "I am

Miguel Harfush," he said, introducing himself and telling us that he was in the group of the hoteliers' convention that had just finished. I found his clean-cut, manly, and educated appearance more than attractive and captivating. He proceeded to interrogate us, wanting to know all about our lives. At the end of his interrogation, Sandy and I felt free to bombard him with questions. Approximately one hour later, Sandy felt tired and went to sleep. Miguel and I stayed chatting until they closed the bar and then went down to the lobby to continue to get to know each other.

Miguel suggested that since my plane was leaving so early the following morning and he had to leave around the same time, it wasn't worth retiring to sleep for not more than two hours. I would have enough hours of sleep on the plane. And he could sleep while his chauffeur drove him back to Melaque— a town 217 miles from Guadalajara on the coast of Jalisco, where he was building a hotel.

Sandy and I agreed that our stay shortened in a breath, with our agenda so busy from our arrival until our last day, with that turbulence of activities, in the end, at least we learned to say *adiós, - tres tacos de carne asada por favor, - un tequila para mí - y ¿cuánto cuesta?* Which translates to *goodbye, - three carne asada tacos please, - one tequila for me -* and *¿how much is it?-* Among the basic grammar and other conversation themes, these were phrases embedded in our minds and, at our return on the plane, I realized that among my chest of beautiful memories of Guadalajara, those main phrases in Spanish that came to stay in my memory wouldn't be of any help wanting to communicate with my students.

FOURTEEN

Two months after my return from Guadalajara, one Thursday evening, climbing the staircase toward the door of my condo, I heard the phone ringing. I ran to reach the phone when I heard Miguel begin to leave a message on my machine. I answered after I heard him saying that he had important news. "I don't want to do it over the phone," he said. "I will arrive tomorrow on Central Airlines flight 236. If the plane gets on time, I'll be there at 5.30 p.m. Make dinner reservations at your favorite restaurant. See you tomorrow."

Taking his offer seriously, I made a reservation at the Flagstaff House. Thrilled about seeing Miguel again, I was intrigued about why he couldn't say what he had to over the phone. I recalled him mentioning in Guadalajara that with the inheritance from his maternal grandfather, he and a group of investors would start building the first 4-star hotel in Melaque. To dabble in the hotel industry was his grandparents' wish, but Miguel liked politics and achieving significant progress for his town. It was on his immediate plans to announce his candidacy for mayor. I gathered he belonged to a reputable family. And he was sure of not having a strong opponent as City Mayor.

Since the night we met in Guadalajara, I felt attracted to Miguel. I liked his personality and tenacity to pursue his goals— I also thought we had many things in common. But the way of showing up in my life without asking me if I had any plans for that weekend bothered me. Buying a plane ticket to visit me without consulting with me beforehand seemed excessive and unorganized.

Delighting the superb menu and the insuperable service of an unforgettable romantic evening gave Miguel the confidence to initiate the conversation. Suddenly, I almost choked on the glass of the expensive Cabernet Sauvignon wine, a perfect pairing to my steak au poivre. Not sure if I'd heard right, I had to interrupt him before he finished talking.

"Did I hear right? Are you proposing to me? We've only seen each other once before, in Guadalajara. From what you've told me, you are already established in Melaque. A place that I don't even know. And I work here. I like my career, and I see possibilities to grow in my profession."

"I understand. But it won't take you more than two days to get acquainted with Melaque. If you're interested in working when my term as mayor ends, you teach English."

"Forgive me, Miguel, but I didn't graduate from the university to be an English teacher. I'm attracted to teaching on each of its facets— teaching, disciplining, and motivating youngsters is not a challenge suitable for everyone, and I feel comfortable doing it. I already initiated my work here in Boulder, and my goal is, with time, to be transferred to Denver to a bigger school, not the opposite."

"I know all of this took you by surprise. But wouldn't you want some time to think about it?"

"I wouldn't be honest to make you wait when I know the

decision is made. We don't know each other well enough. There's still a lot to discover about each other. I'm attracted to you, but I'm not prepared for matrimony. I'm sorry."

"I think you're not giving yourself or me the opportunity."

"And I think we should not continue with this topic. I'm flattered and grateful to you. But I'm pretty sure this wouldn't work."

Breaking the heart of someone who had deposited all his hopes on a project is not easy. But marriage is more than a project. If, in the beginning, I felt attracted to Miguel, the easiest and fastest way to get rid of that feeling was his craziness. To not wait for the right time and push things in such a manner. Besides, I like to go to theaters and fancy restaurants, wear designer clothes, and live in a sophisticated world. How would my life be in a town where the only attraction is contemplating the stars? NO. Life goes on, and I want to continue living. It doesn't matter if I'm not the first lady in a town with nothing to do but wait for a high tide.

Six months later, on a Sunday, early in the morning before eight, my cell phone rang off the hook. I had no intention of answering. My plan for the day was to keep sleeping but whoever was calling was not giving up and was not leaving a message either.

Half asleep, I answered, prepared to put the person interrupting my rest with so much perseverance in his place.

"My dearest friend, nice of you to finally answer."

"Sandy? Why on this earth are you calling me on Sunday before eight o'clock in the morning? Not even you get up this early."

"I know. But today I'm so excited I couldn't sleep. I had to tell you this because I want you to be the first one to know it."

"To know what? Woman. You already woke me up. So tell

me once and for all— what's going on with you?"

"Well, the thing is that Joel proposed to me last night. I wish you had seen it. It was like a fairy tale. I didn't see it coming."

"Wait! You're talking too fast. Give me all the details— I want to know it all."

"Those, I'll give them to you later because he's picking me up at nine to take me to breakfast. But I didn't want to go without telling you before. I need you to start planning your trip. I will get married in the Spring of next year, and I want you to be my maid of honor. I would never forgive you if you were not part of my wedding party."

"And I would never forgive you if you would not ask me to." But before, tell me, are you sure about this marriage? You met him four months ago. Do you believe you know him well enough? Besides, being a doctor's wife is never easy. I'm happy for you, but more than anything, I want you to feel that this is THE ONE, that your happiness will last a lifetime."

"I feel like I've known him forever. I assure you that this is the one I've been waiting for. I will call you tonight. We have lots of planning to do and a lot to talk about. I love you."

"And I love you too. Congratulations. And thank you for sharing this news with me."

"My mind spun around, imagining that from that instant, my life would not be the same— Sandy and I had shared so many happy moments, all of those trips that left unforgettable memories, and all of that would end with my dearest friend's wedding."

"What an irony! The two of us were proposed in the same year, and there will be one wedding only. And after losing the opportunity to marry, will I also lose my best friend now? Of course not! The friendship between Sandy and I doesn't grow in pots. More than friends, we are like sisters. And that lasts a lifetime. Sandy is like a sister to me except that we don't fight with each other, and I must feel fortunate that instead of losing a friend, I'm gaining a brother who, besides, is a doctor. Nothing like having one in the family."

After the fourth year of working at the school in Boulder, Colorado, a job opportunity opened in Denver. I applied for it, confident about my experience and the ability to pursue my goals. I didn't complete the semester. Once they found the right person for my replacement, they asked me to move to Denver. Being this a more prestigious school, they had an extreme urgency to fill the vacancy that the previous teacher suddenly left due to health issues.

Since my first visit to Colorado on a ski trip a few years before, we flew to Denver. And I've been fond of the city since then. When I accepted my job in Boulder, it was not exactly what I was looking for. But there was an opportunity, and I decided to take it as the first step to gaining experience, thinking I would remain in Boulder for a couple of years, and before I realized it, it had been four years.

I was assigned to that grade that most teachers wouldn't want. The senior in high school and I had to put up with all kinds of situations among teenagers— starting with the ones that didn't pass if they didn't copy, the ones that skipped class to smoke marijuana, the couples in love that missed classes looking for a refuge to hide and be away from everyone, and even the older boys who found me attractive and tried to call my attention, thinking that after some persistence I would fall into their games. But by then, teacher Katya was smart enough to discipline adolescents, and any stone on the way, I moved it away with such a skill that it became clear to my students who established the game rules.

Each time there was an opportunity, two of my friends and I, who shared a passion for skiing, would get away to a ski resort in Vail. With time, I improved to the point of impressing with my achievements. On one occasion, while my friends took a break on one of the intermediate mountains, someone approached me when I was waiting for the ski lift.

"Do you mind if we share?" He asked me with an accent that I identified as Middle Eastern. I didn't know what race he was, but I didn't bother finding out. Right away, I answered affirmatively. His eyes and charm captivated me from the moment he asked me to share the ski lift. We talked for less than five minutes, but before we said goodbye, he asked to meet me at the bar at the entrance around 5:00 p.m.

Skiing all day long with resting intervals to meet my friends, at 5:00 p.m. sharp, relaxed with glasses of wine in our hands, the three of us waited, intrigued to know if my Middle Eastern prince would show up. Punctually he confirmed his intention. He arrived with his cousin, and after the introductions and talking until the stomach reminded us it was time to compensate it with food, Zayed— that was my friend's name of Arab origin, invited us to dinner at his place.

The door opened, and my friends and I entered, gawking at the opulence and the number of people working in the house to service that vacation spot, where the owner showed up barely three times during the Winter season. At Zayed's service were two security guards, one chauffeur, two housekeepers, a chef, and a general maintenance worker.

Delighted on an exquisite dinner which, perhaps, our hedonistic pleasures wouldn't have allowed us to experience at any of the best restaurants in Vail, we listened to Zayed, who said he lived in Abu Dhabi, the Capital of the Arab Emirates. In the summer, he traveled to his house in Miami. And, in Winter, to Vail. Not wanting to provide more details, he mentioned another property in France. Dying out of curiosity but not to make it obvious, we didn't go deeper into questions.

The next day, we met again at the ski slopes. At five p.m., we repeated the bar gathering, followed by dinner at his place.

Sadly, I saw my love story come to an end. Zayed promised to come back at the first opportunity. In the meantime, he called me frequently. Although he gave me his cell phone number, he showed his preference since the beginning for being the one who called me, arguing that his European car import business kept him busy most of the time.

Our relationship lasted about fourteen months, during which, despite the distance, I felt more attracted, and the attraction turned into love, the kind that needs to have the loved one by our side. Then Sandy opened my eyes.

"Katya, I love you dearly. And I want the best for you. But have you thought about the direction your relationship with Zayed is taking?"

"I don't know, Sandy, but I don't want to pressure him."

"I understand. And I think you're acting with common sense. But don't you agree that you should have a conversation with him to know you're not on thin ice? I don't want to disappoint you. But you don't know his family. What if they don't accept you for being from another country, having different beliefs, and another religion, and what if they have chosen his future wife? I don't know much about their customs, but I heard that some of their matrimonies are prearranged."

"You're right. I'll take the risk and have a serious talk with Zayed."

I thought about Sandy's conversation for a long time, until I got the courage to talk to Zayed about it, aware of what I was risking.

"Zayed, I need to ask you something. Please, you must answer me honestly. We haven't talked about the future, about your point of view on a family and whatever it is, I will understand, but I need to know. Have your parents chosen a wife for you in Abu Dhabi?"

"The things that go through your mind, Katya. Of course not. I choose my wives, as I've chosen my two actual wives, but if that marriage issue worries you, we can get married. I know how independent you are, but I assure you, you will have everything with me here".

"Wait a moment! Did you say you have two wives, and the two live in the same house? And I would live there too? Excuse me, don't bother to answer. I should've known since the beginning that all of this was too good to be true. I love you, but it is best if you don't call me again. Dedicate instead to finding your third wife somewhere else. Traveling in the same bus with all the members of the rock band between presentations is not my thing."

FIFTEEN

Mariana

My Papa Jimmy's health continued to deteriorate fast. He hardly ate. Everyone at home concluded that his days were numbered, and while I refused to accept the reality, my mom kept on searching for love among the wrong men and depriving my dad of the time the belonged to only him since he was at the end of his life. Although, aware of my mom's behavior, he still loved her with the same intensity and greater need for her love, of her showing him at least a little gratitude, and of how important he had always been to us.

My mom and I were in debt with my dad. He helped us to know a different side of life in every possible way. But the weight leaned toward me, paying my debt alone because my mom saw it as a given thing that soon, her husband wouldn't be with us anymore, and she took a step ahead, starting to live her widowhood.

His admission to the hospital became imminent. His organs gradually failed, and he could not eat by himself. Losing significant weight, his physical appearance surprisingly worsened. He was only suffering, and under those circumstances, we could think he was prepared to leave this world, but if he was ready, the question was— was I willing to accept the inevitable?

My desire to live vanished at fourteen years old, without this being the first time. The pain continued piling up uncontrollably. My Papa Jimmy had already passed, and I selfishly kept longing for his presence, even knowing that despite being alive he had no life. It blurred after the stroke.

Indescribable pain seizes me each time I remember him paralyzed on one half of his body and having lost his strength, power, and dignity. My mom and I bathed, dressed, and fed him. Although most of the time, it was me who did it, that never bothered me. Despite his condition, he transmitted love with his sight and comforted me. He was the only man who could've seen me as a father, with that relationship between adult and child that implies respect, love, good example, and protection. Thanks to him, I learned to live my life with confidence and no fear, as any child with a father capable of fighting against adversity to protect his family.

When my Papa Jimmy came into my life to stay, for the first time, I desired to live. I liked to feel loved and that someone worried about me, and I felt safe next to him. God is my witness that I was consumed by grief seeing my dad experiencing pain in such a way after that stroke that transformed his last days into suffering. But even like that, I needed his presence, although he could no longer speak to me. I was deeply fond of him and wanted to imagine he would live forever, but that was asking for too much. It meant wanting to change the destiny of what was written. I was also feeding my ego, wishing to have my dad by my side and witnessing the pain his health condition caused him.

On a gray Winter morning, when the birds migrate searching for the sun, waiting for the Spring, and we cannot hear their singing, when everything feels gloomy, and the flowers don't show their first signs of life, my Papa Jimmy's heart stopped beating.

My loneliness then weighed more than a hundred pounds of cement. I missed my dad. My grandmother had moved and lived in a warehouse with a group of people, all of them bonded by alcohol consumption. I also longed for my grandma because I knew that she loved me. In her way and with her alcohol addiction, she could never do much for me. Still, to every extent possible, she protected me. She interfered between my mother and Eustolio, the musician with whom we previously lived, every time they wanted to beat me— being my grandma, the one who often received the blows coming in my direction, so that after, they would end up with me and, in the end, I didn't escape either from a good kicking.

Also, my grandma opposed the times they tried to tie me. Because she was weaker, mostly when my mom and Eustolio teamed up, the dragon inside them could not be stopped. However, as soon as they got distracted, Grandma tried the impossible to untie me, knowing that she would later pay for her act of insubordination.

Loneliness and sadness were wearing me down, but there was something else consuming me— the regret of not having done anything to prevent abuse to my grandma, the same abuse I took part in as a child when my mother pushed me to those mistreats. I obeyed her for fear of her thrashings.

Grandma was never a mean person. Her only wish was to live to drink and to lose consciousness afterward. I was just a child to know the origins of that addiction that accompanied her until the end of her days. At my age, I didn't understand many things. We could say that I didn't understand anything. I only survived, sometimes even against my wishes, I continued doing it. And perhaps, the two of us, without being close to each other, felt close, identified by suffering, by the absence of enthusiasm about tomorrow, and by that bond developed among victims— each of us living in different circumstances but both with a similar seed, rejection of a life that gave us scant opportunities to discover its good side, that side that neither my grandma nor I could hold on to, by lack of knowledge and loneliness.

How hard it is to think that fate, on its constant wandering, does not allow us to go back to the past opportunities— now, with maturity, I would've liked to talk to my grandma to know about the root that grew damaged inside her. I would have wanted to tell her that I loved her, although I could never show it. But she's gone, and I realized that despite my immense child suffering, thanks to her, this was slightly lighter. I don't want to imagine what my life would have been like if I had been alone with my mom.

Now that I found myself alone with my mother, I knew I didn't want to continue living with her. There were too many scars, not only engraved but embossed in my heart. Loneliness terrified me, but it did more to continue living with my mom and the pain she caused me since I was a child when the musician she lived with abused me. Although she didn't know it until the end, the one thing she was aware of was that that man hit me for no reason, and my mom allowed it, igniting the fire by taking part in those unfair punishments with the only goal of pleasing that person, who was a stranger to our family.

I had my reasons to bear a grudge— seeing the injustice toward my grandma, being treated with such little dignity all the time, with the lack of respect and patience that we owe to the elderly because once they go, don't look for a moment to say goodbye, they suddenly disappear one day. And we never see them again, nor have the opportunity to ask them to forgive our faults and to express them a sign of affection. They disappear as a balloon in the sky that, in an instant, escapes from our hands, and we see it flying away until we lose sight of it and never see it again.

Bad blood kept growing inside me. Not a day passed without me feeling remorse, but it was more than that. The sense of guilt had weighed on me since childhood due to the sexual abuse I was a victim of. And I kept asking myself if I provoked it. I had no orientation from my mom or any adult. But above all, my bitterness leaned toward her. Carrying my secret for fear of her reaction made me feel insecure and abandoned. I considered myself dirty and lost, trying to hide my shame from my friends and schoolmates, fearing the one day when the truth would come out and that everyone would reject me, seeing me as someone inferior.

I also regretted not having been able to have a family with sisters and cousins and all kinds of relatives to play with. I continuously reproached life for giving me a father to take him away later without warning when I felt happy to have him by my side, thinking my happiness would last forever. And by taking him, it left me with the tortuous memories of his final days. I remember the unbearable pain the day the bullet crossed my chest, and I felt asphyxiated regardless of how big my effort trying to breathe, but now it asphyxiates me more the expression of horror on his face, not being able to stop me from shooting that gun and knowing what would come afterward.

Now that I talk to him on my lonely nights, I ask for his forgiveness for all the grief my confused child mind caused him. I only thought about accomplishing my plan of ending my rocky road that became more challenging each time. And in my depressive thoughts, there was a place for one only— To dominate my fear of doubting for an instant and not having the strength to continue with my elaborated plan, assembling each piece with precision to make them fit perfectly and not to leave anything out of what according to me, would end up instantly my meaningless life.

My plan worked, but despite my efforts to study it carefully to achieve a perfect result, it worked halfway because, above all the physical and psychological pain, my heart was still beating, despite having placed a revolver on my chest destined to shoot a bullet directly to my heart and end up instantly with my life. I'm still alive. The doctors and nurses played the role of my enemies, and in the end, they were the ones who won this battle. That made me think that no matter how hard I tried to stop living, fate had a different plan for me.

After a few months, terrified, I discovered that the plan that destiny had in store for me was to continue living since my time hadn't come yet, and that depressed me more each day. I did not accept my fate that stood between my desire to end up with the suffering I had endured since my childhood, which became heavier over time. But something that had been part of my personality since I was a little girl was pursuing my goals without paying attention to obstacles.

Without thinking more about the stones that could appear on my path, I decided to concentrate on a new plan that would give me a reason to get up every morning, to achieve it above any adversity.

SIXTEEN

One night at the quinceañera party of my friend Malú, I lived a different experience, one more of the many I had been experiencing in the last year. Splurge would be the right word to describe the party Cesar, Malú's boyfriend, organized for her. He rented a salon, which I knew later was reserved a year in advance by a couple to celebrate their silver wedding anniversary. I was still too young to understand how my friend's boyfriend had managed one month before to get that salon that a while back had been secured by someone else.

They hired a band from Sinaloa. And a local group played during the band's breaks. They served birria, a typical Mexican beef stew made with goat. The menu also included a variety of appetizers and a five-tier cake with a fondant figure at the top, wearing the same dress as the quinceañera. The party lasted until 4 a.m. to finish with mariachi, and the second round on the menu included menudo.

Beer and liquor circulated as if it was the night before the prohibition. But that was not the only thing circulating in that room— Malú's and Selena's boyfriends made rolls of marijuana and passed them around. By the time Carlos Alberto passed me the joint, I didn't have time to react, and before I knew it, I was smoking.

Arriving home, I went straight to bed. Three hours later, my mom woke me up with her screams. She became furious the moment she detected the marijuana smell on my clothes. This only increased the water in the glass that was about to spill. She didn't want me to continue seeing Carlos Alberto or my friends. Unfortunately, none of them knew what they were getting into, and they kept falling deeper.

Since that evening, the marijuana affair became something regular. Drinking became more frequent and later a daily habit. Not much longer after, on a Sunday afternoon, Malú invited Carlos Alberto and me to a carne asada at her place, and without hesitation, we confirmed our attendance.

That was the first time we snorted cocaine with the rest of the group. I felt intimidated at the beginning to know how easily I was falling deeper into drugs, and at that point, my internal war started since I had no intention of stopping. I felt like I had the world at my feet and could achieve anything. It was a well-being sensation I hadn't felt before. On that afternoon, I also discovered at Cesar's house that he had a gun. Noticing my expression of fear, he winked cynically. "It's for protection." He said, "Don't be afraid."

A few days later, Malú said she was unworried. Everyone in that group had guns, and what I saw that Sunday was a toy compared to what she'd seen one day in Cesar's closet. I was curious and scared, and I asked her where Cesar worked and why he had guns. She was unsure. He seemed to work for the police or something like that, but she didn't ask him because he disliked touching that subject.

On one of Carlos Alberto's breaks, I had a conversation with him that I hadn't had before. I started by asking him if he owned a gun, to which he answered affirmatively. Due to his job, it was necessary to learn how to use it with precision, and there was a place for those who wanted where they could pay to have this kind of training. I also asked him if he knew his three friends had firearms because that scared me. And it made me uncomfortable.

"No reason to worry. I think differently. I believe it's good to have those types of friends since they are untouchable and powerful, and if we don't mess with them, they will never mess with us. On the contrary, we will be protected."

"I don't know if we are doing the right thing. I like that sensation that cocaine and amphetamines cause— it excites me to be energetic, alert, and with power. And the pleasure of not having inhibitions when I'm under the influence of ecstasies are feelings that I only experience with these drugs."

"You said the keywords, not having inhibitions. I adore seeing you like that."

"And I love feeling that way, but I wonder when we could deviate from the auto-destructive path we are heading. What if, one day, things get out of control and the addiction takes over us?"

"You shouldn't worry about it. This is temporary. We'll leave it soon because if they detect me at work, I can lose my job, which isn't my goal. One day, I want to be someone important. I know I can do it. Besides, working for the US government has many benefits. As time goes by, you will notice it. For now, what I like is the respect people treat you with, and if the United States goes to war with another country and you're deployed, if you make it alive, upon your return, everybody sees you as a hero. It's a feeling of pride, hard to put into words."

"I wouldn't know what to do if they deploy you to fight in another country."

"You would do the same as all the girlfriends and wives of Navy guys in this situation— wait anxiously for our return to enjoy every minute of every day we're together."

"I think you're right. But there's something else that still bothers me. The boyfriends of Rosita and Selena, where do they work? Are they policemen also?"

"It's unclear. Malú says her boyfriend works for the Judicial Police, but that's what he says because it hasn't been proven. And as for Rosita's and Selena's boyfriends, they are... let's say, merchants."

"Of?"

"Mariana, why do you ask so many questions?"

"Because I need to know."

"Do you need, or do you want?"

"I need to know. They are not as cool as they were in the beginning. They are arrogant. I don't know. They frighten me."

"Well, I guess I don't need to answer. If that's what you think, there you have your answer. Besides, where do you think the drugs we use are coming from? It is always convenient to have a close connection. That way, we can get our merchandise whenever we want."

"I'm under the impression things could go south in the end. I found Malú crying the other day with bruises on her face. It was Cesar."

"I'm not justifying him, but that's between them. All I can tell you is that if you never betray Cesar, Felipe, or Raymundo, they won't mess with you or harm you in any way— on the contrary, everybody fears them. And, as long as we're friends with them, nobody will dare to hurt us."

"And what about you? Have you ever dealt drugs?"

"How can you even mention it? I told you that I'm happy with my job. That's my future, and I will leave the drugs soon. I'm aware of the risk I'm taking. If they discover it in the Navy, they will instantly fire me. I don't want to continue doing this much longer."

"Sometimes, I also wish to leave them. Suddenly, I reflect on my life, and I feel bad— so much alcohol. All those drugs,

I feel a great emptiness, and every time, I'm more frightened, thinking that one day it might be too late to stop."

"For now, we're having fun. When the time comes, we'll see how we can get out of this together."

"And do you think that my friends will be able to get out one day if they want to? They are too deep into this, and when they are sober, and I speak with them, the three express the same fear of not knowing what their boyfriends are capable of."

"They might be scared, but I see how much they enjoy the purses and expensive presents they receive, and they also like to arrive at restaurants where their boyfriends spend limitlessly."

"I don't know. I'm under the impression that things are not as they seem."

Those days were not the best in my life. All that euphoria and well-being sensation that we experienced with drugs when I was high, the moment I stopped, I fell brutally, and when I descended, the depression invaded me. In those moments, when I saw a reflection of myself in the mirror, not only did I see an unknown girl, but the deep sight entered too far inside me until I met that soiled soul. I recalled the last days of my Papa Jimmy, during which I tried to avoid eye contact. I didn't want him to notice what I was doing. It's hard to know if he was aware of my behavior. There was something strange in his expression. I didn't spend much time with him as before either, talking to him and showing him my love, not because I didn't love him as much, but out of fear that he would discover how low I'd fallen with my actions.

Over time, I realized that the victim's language is not something we learn. We identify it, and it makes us close to one another, creating a sisterhood of an indistinguishable root.

My friends and I felt related to each other a few years ago. And we became inseparable since then— three of us with a similar current of abuse and Rosita, allied by the suffering different from Malú's, Selena's, and mine but with the same lack of hope we grew up under.

Rosita was born and lived in a different core family. We all grew up in poverty, but she had loving parents willing to do anything needed to raise their children. Nevertheless, their efforts were in vain trying to help Ramon, Rosita's brother, who suffered from a degenerative disease that consumed his muscles from an early age.

Ramon worked at an auto parts store but was fired when his muscles began to lose strength. He could not lift any heavy box or anything else with a certain weight for as minimum as it was. And he could not reach the parts stored on the higher shelves either. Seeing himself without a job, he opted to sell windshield wipers at Tecate International Border. Occasionally, he sold window shades and microfiber car cleaning clothes.

Ramon used to work from an early age. He went to school and worked afterward. Two of his sisters did the same, and with their parent's income and theirs, they lived comfortably, satisfying their basic needs. Ramon's disease progressed rapidly, and the problem was easily detected by the people crossing the border frequently.

The ideal combination of sympathy and pity for a young, handsome, hard-working guy whose health declined with giant steps pushed a significant number of people crossing the border to spare some coins at first and later a bill, even without buying anything, and, as his illness advanced, his income increased. His hands started to deform, he could hardly speak, and his feet ended up inverted in a way that prevented him from walking. By then, he was famous in Tecate. People saw him from far away when crossing and switched lanes to stretch one arm and toss a bill in Ramon's nosebag.

DOMINANCE DELUSIONS

The surprise in Rosita's family grew, seeing the income that a young man whose body had started to deform could generate. The economic situation, more comfortable each time, led to increasing frustration of his parents and sisters not being able to do anything despite having the means to stop the spread of this disease. Everyone agreed on wanting to live in poverty in exchange for each family member to have mental and physical health.

Rosita was the youngest. Going through the whimsical stage of adolescence was affected the most, and she did not hesitate to fall into the destructive world of drugs to later fall deeper into her addiction.

Selena and Malú shared the injustice of abuse from an early age— Malú, the sexual abuse, and Selena the physical that at certain times, the parents, due to financial, social, or moral deficiencies, reflect their frustration, mistreating their children and without being aware that no adult has that right regarding minors.

On the other side, I had the complete package, having been tied, beaten, and sexually abused as a child. Because of that, I felt linked to this group of friends. None of them worried about falling deeper into their abyss. Neither alcohol nor drugs. And they turned into an addiction. Besides, one of us was disoriented, and the other three, with a profound need for love, found it among the wrong people. Malú, Selena, and Rosita clung to their partners without knowing that mistakes can occasionally be amended. But sometimes, we don't have that opportunity and don't realize it until the cause is lost.

My situation was different due to the fast pace of my life. Far ahead in every aspect and with an intelligence rarely found in a girl my age. I was in love with Carlos Alberto, and to my advantage, at least my boyfriend had a decent job. If he decided to continue going on the right track, and we were still together, our future would be financially and socially secure.

My three friends and I loved with that teenage adoration that makes one think it is impossible to love more. Despite all the wrong things a partner might have, we could not leave him, imagining that if that relationship ends, we will never love another person again, not knowing that at that age, it is just the beginning and often, is necessary to go through that and many more disappointments and heartaches before finding the right person that will bring us eternal happiness.

With this mentality, my friends not only tried to hide and keep inside their boyfriends' abuse but accepted the risks they were exposed to by being linked to the wrong people. And if they wanted to keep their eyes closed and not be aware of playing with fire, I did detect the danger. Fear and impossibility made me insecure. Despite being in love with Carlos Alberto, I could sense he wasn't the perfect man for me. However, I accepted him regardless of his defects, knowing that perfection in a human being doesn't exist and with the hope that those things that made me anxious would diminish over time.

Unlike everyone in the group, who depended more on alcohol and drugs each day, there was a time when I started to get tired of them. I felt good when I used them, but still, I was unhappy with my life and needed a change.

Seeing myself on a dead-end frightened me. Seeing that my friends had no way out worried me even more. Not being able to do anything about it started to derail me. Although Carlos Alberto was with me, the absurd yet familiar feeling devoured me— life had no meaning, and I wanted to end it. I'd already tried before. And if this time I studied my plan carefully, I would succeed.

I kept witnessing life without meaning, without goals on my friends' side, and the danger that kept wrapping them like an hourglass. And I felt more tired of being part of that shifting swamp from which no one could escape. Alcohol and drugs turned my stomach, and my life provoked the same effect on me. In my mind, I had one goal, even contradictory, that was the only thing that helped me to continue living— to find a way to end my existence.

It had been three years since my suicide attempt. The intense pain that oppressed my chest and didn't let me breathe was still vivid in my memory. The idea of shooting myself was discharged. I knew there was a possibility of the bullet finding its way to exit my body, or it could've been extracted as it was the first time, and in the end, having the courage or the cowardice to do it for no reason made me reconsider it the next time.

For some time, I thought about poisoning myself, but with what? What was the exact dose, and how or where did one get it? That was a complicated plan. I had previously heard about people who let themselves die. Then again, the question arose— how does someone die purposely? Stop eating, perhaps? That would be a long process. If I was to do it, I needed to do it effectively and fast.

The chain of doubts kept on growing. And the idea was to stop living and thinking. Things were not easy, and one day, as in a cloud of dreams, the answer came to me. The thought suddenly appeared. And afterward, I was wrapped in peace, knowing I'd finally found the solution I'd been looking for quite some time.

Carlos Alberto was, like most of the time, at the ship. And that would make things easier. His absence gave me the strength needed to continue with my plan.

It was 6.45 p.m. on Tuesday, November 12th. The days started getting shorter, and by 6 p.m., daylight disappeared. In the darkness, it would be easier to reach my goal. No one would interfere.

My heart was full of sorrow, my palm hands sweating, my bewildered mind, and the desire to end up once and for all with my meaningless life pushed me to accelerate my steps to a darkened corner. Lifting my gaze briefly, I calculated the distance strategically and ran.

I threw myself into a car that came in the opposite direction to land on the cold asphalt several steps away, with a powerful hit in the left part of my body, the femur outside my leg, still feeling an uncontrollable pain, and suddenly, I started to see everything dark, everything blurry, everything cold.

SEVENTEEN

Two days after they took me to the hospital, being conscious but still weak and tired from the medication, I opened my eyes, and I saw Carlos Alberto sitting next to my bed.

"I came as soon as I could. The commander officer didn't want to let me out, but I told him I had a family emergency. I will probably have to stay on the ship on my next break."

"Who told you?"

"Who do you think? Selena, who was sober for the first time in a while."

"She hasn't been here, nor any of my friends."

"It seems like your visits are restricted. They didn't want to let me in either. I told them I wouldn't return to San Diego without seeing you. They hardly let me in. But they warned me that it could be only for a few minutes."

"I don't know if I will ever walk again. I have several fractures on my leg, mainly on a bone called the femur, and I believe that now my left leg will be slightly shorter than the right."

"Why did you do it, Mariana? I thought you loved me and

were happy with our relationship."

"Of course I love you. It's my life that I didn't want."

"And what about all those plans that we made together? You were going to abandon me without saying a word. Do you have a slight idea of the suffering you would have caused me if you had not survived?"

"Forgive me. You know how much I love you, and the last thing I would do is hurt you, but I've been carrying an unbearable weight. I didn't want to continue drinking and, above all, taking drugs. I was desperate to stop doing all that, but I didn't know how to get out."

"Wouldn't it have been easier to talk to me instead of trying to kill yourself?"

"I tried to tell you several times. But I saw you were very deep into this addiction. Besides, that was not the only reason. It was my life that I've always seen as despicable."

Taking both of my hands softly, so as not to hurt my left one where I had a syringe inserted to administer the intravenous serum, Carlos Alberto tried to penetrate my eyes of that hazel color he was in love with, and with how they communicated, even speechless, they said a thousand things with my deep expression exploding with the slightest feeling.

"Look, I won't promise you anything, but I can assure you that if that drug matter bothers you that much, I will try to use them less until the time comes when we stop them for good. But in exchange, I need you to promise me that you will never do anything of such nature again. If you ever feel desperate, before making any hasty decision like this, talk to me first, and together we'll find a solution. Do you promise?"

"I will do whatever you want me to. But I need some time. I need to know what direction my life is taking."

"Your life will follow the path you want to give it. It's like the ship where I work. If you want to switch course, all you got to do is change the direction of the rudder."

"I don't get it."

"Don't worry if you don't for now. With time, you will. I must go. I can't stay here too long, but rest assured I will come back at the first chance. And please, if you don't see me for a few days, don't get alarmed. I will try to work overtime to be here on your birthday."

"How did you remember?"

"How would I not? You will turn fifteen years old in three weeks. You told me so on the day I met you at that house you took care of. The day you threatened me with that rifle."

"I didn't threaten you. You know I was playing."

"Yes. But those little games of yours sometimes scare me."

Three weeks later, one of the nurses came for me and took me in a wheelchair to a room. I don't know what part of the hospital it was, but the first thing I saw on our arrival was a big sign that read, *Happy Birthday, Mariana.* They brought me a cake, and one of the nurses gave me a blessed medal of Saint Francis of Assisi. "This medal will protect you forever," she said. "If you have faith, you have no idea of the miracles Saint Francis of Assisi can do for you."

My three friends were also there, and each one showed up with a present but, of them all, the most important to me was the medal and a silver chain with a heart that Carlos Alberto gave me. He was the last one to leave, and his shows of love were endless. He wanted to stay and not leave me for a minute.

"Do you agree that it wasn't hard to make it to your fifteenth birthday? Why were you trying to avoid it and end your life three weeks before?"

"It wasn't about making it to fifteen. I was trying to avoid the fifteenth and sixteenth and any future birthdays. You know what my life has been like. I have nothing that makes me proud and a lot to be ashamed of. Besides, I already told you— I was tired of everything. And I didn't find another way out."

"And now, do you still feel the same way? I saw you in excellent spirits, and that's how I like to see you."

"I feel different. Everyone at the hospital has been wonderful to me, and I'm starting to see things through another light."

"Well, I gotta go. Tomorrow, I have to leave by four and be at 6 a.m. on the ship. Very Happy Birthday again. Let's hope we celebrate many more together."

"Thank you for having been with me today. I think you were right. It was indeed a happy birthday. It would've been foolish not to experience this day when I felt so appreciated and realized how many people care about me."

"Starting with?"

"My boyfriend, who's the most handsome of all."

"Now your intelligence and good taste for men are obvious. At least, today, we agree on something."

My mom arrived after everyone had left, arguing that she was working. I believe she did it to avoid my friends and my boyfriend. If she hadn't seen them with good eyes before, now, after what I did, she seemed to detest them.

Three more weeks passed, and then one month, and another one, and at the end of the third, they released me from the hospital. Although I was limping, I could walk. I resumed my physical therapy, and due to not being in a coma state this time, my psychological rehabilitation started almost instantaneously from my checking in the hospital. I had plenty of things to reflect on, one of them— to have been hit by a car and continue living, and simultaneously, a bus passed and managed to avoid me. And even though I had several fractures on my left leg, I was still alive.

Why was I still in this world after two suicide attempts carefully planned so that if the first one failed, there was no reason for the second to go wrong? And for the most part, after the shocking blow I received. That was my first question, and although, in the beginning, I adamantly refused to continue being part of this world, now, I was aware of my limitations. My time had not come yet. One thing I was sure of was a change in me because now I knew that my actions in the previous months were the cause of my disgust and made me sick. And I was the only one who could initiate that much-needed change.

With that mindset, I left the hospital, and I swore never to return to my addictions. I stayed away from drugs. Those three months, when I focused on my physical rehabilitation, helped me to detox my body and soul. The previous stimulation that could become deadly was never my thing, and the alcohol wouldn't lead me to anything good either. If before, I longed to belong in that group of friends, now I couldn't find a powerful reason to force something into my body that I disliked. What not only made me cheerful but forced me to advance more each time was the bicycle, which was essential for my total rehabilitation.

The welfare sensation of pedaling a bicycle contributed to my dedication to that activity. The memory of the first time I used one jumped into my mind, and I lost myself in time until the therapist reminded me it was time to stop. Thanks to those therapies and my dedication to them, my limpness became imperceptible.

The frayed tempers of Carlos Alberto and I seemed to deteriorate before my admittance to the hospital, but in my release, the change was impressive. Now, he was loving, tried to please me in every way, and with great effort diminished the alcohol consumption, which was hard when being surrounded by our friends who now we saw less frequently.

Of my three friends, Rosita was the one who insisted on seeing each other more often. She and I had been friends since the first grade. Together, we went through all the shades of experiences that life could've given us. Although I loved her deeply, my pain of seeing her falling into that ocean of suffering from which it would be hard to come afloat one day was as deep.

Selena's physical abuse by her boyfriend became more evident, as it was also clear that she continued sinking into the drug habit. That caused her negligence in her physical appearance— she was two years older than me, and at seventeen, her health and beauty started to decline.

While my friends kept on following the wrong path, I tried to focus on my studies and to keep my purpose of not looking back and never returning to the bad times that led me to pursue the end of my meaningless life, to achieve my goal I saw the need to draw a line between my friends who refused to leave their decadent world.

Separating from my friends more each time, five months after my hospital release, produced the opposite effect on my relationship with Carlos Alberto. We were in love and surrendered to each other, and he was not only dedicated to me, but he also fixated on the job that he loved more every day.

I wished I'd never seen the day arrive, but I knew it could happen any time, and one night, after returning from the movies, he told me he would be deployed to the Philippines in two more weeks.

EIGHTEEN

Seven months, two weeks, and three days later, the ship leaving the Philippines reached the port of San Diego, where Carlos Alberto came, among other sailors. At 10 a.m., I was ready, wearing a one-shoulder fuchsia pink straight dress and my long, loose hair, as he liked. Jewels never interested me, but the heart he gave me on my fifteenth birthday I used on every special occasion, which was every time we went out, and that was the first thing I wore before I started applying my usual natural-looking makeup. Feeling desperate for not having a passport and not meeting him in San Diego on his arrival, the minutes turned endless.

    Around 2 p.m., he showed up at my house and took me to lunch. In his absence, I turned sixteen, and he celebrated his twenty-first birthday on board. He looked more handsome. Although twenty-one is just a number representing a transition in a man's life, the change was notorious to me. I perceived a physical maturity that I hadn't noticed before. It was a happy day. After lunch, he took me shopping with him in Tijuana since he wanted to update his wardrobe slightly. He also bought me a dress and a pair of shoes. And after a delightful day, at nightfall, we loved each other like never before. My happiness was complete. He wrapped me in his tenderness, and from that moment on, we didn't want to separate ever.

Many more followed that ceaselessly happy night. Our days felt eternal. We desperately awaited the evening to welcome the darkness and to make love to each other, wishing our nights of romance had no end.

Submerged in the obsession of not wanting to separate, we lost track of time. Our days passed as in those fast-turning page calendars of the movies, tearing off one sheet and another with unnoticeable quickness, and, on a morning, after two months of Carlos Alberto's return, at the clothing store where I was working, I felt nausea that made me run to the bathroom to turn my stomach, I realized then that it had been six weeks since my last period. I was never behind for more than five days. At that time, I didn't know what kind of test I could have to be 100% sure, but a young, healthy woman knows that when her period stops unexpectedly, in most cases, inevitably, the cause is always the same.

Scared at the beginning, I tried to avoid Carlos Alberto. I was not prepared to tell him, and I feared his reaction. In these times, and at that age, couples are not prepared for parenthood. The days passed, and the secret I continued hiding was eating me alive. I wanted to share it with someone, but the fear of spreading the news forced me to keep quiet. I looked unsuccessfully for the right moment to tell him. When I was about to do it, the cowardice and fear of losing him and that he would leave me abandoned with the immense responsibility that we didn't have time to plan, prevented me from unburdening myself until I noticed the change in my body. And I had no other option than to reveal the truth.

Although liberated from that heavy weight, Carlos Alberto's reaction oppressed my heart. I would've wished he hugged me, made my fear go away, and told me we were in this together, and together with our baby, we would share the future. But sometimes, there's no relationship between what we wish and what happens. Lost, I didn't know what to think. I expected anger and wanted love and understanding, but something that never crossed my mind was indifference.

After a prolonged silence, my anxiety grew like an uncontrollable fire. And, after listening to the words I never expected, I thought my head was about to explode.

"Mariana, I don't know what to say. You know I adore you, but I never saw this coming. You're sixteen years old. Do you feel ready to be a mother? Because I still have many plans for my life, and none of them include to start changing diapers."

"What are you trying to tell me? That you don't want our baby to be born?"

"No. That's not what I meant. I need time to assimilate this. Let me think about the best solution, and we will talk in a couple of days to calm down, and together, we will decide what's best for the three of us."

"What's the best? I think there's not much to think about. We're having a baby. That's crystal clear to me. What is it that we need to think about?"

"If you are convinced to have this baby."

"Of course, I'm convinced. You know I'm catholic. I'm not in favor of abortion."

"As I said, let's calm down and think carefully. We will resume this talk in a few days. For now, it's late, and I must go. Please don't worry and don't make hasty decisions. We'll get out of this together in the best possible manner."

When he said, "let's talk in a couple of days." He didn't mention that in the meantime, we wouldn't see each other, and after four days, I felt I was loosing my mind, and the nausea and discomfort increased. I didn't recall ever feeling worse before. Imagining I had lost my baby's father, I couldn't find a solution to bring peace of mind to my life and help me to carry that weight that seemed impossible I could do alone.

After four days of absence, he appeared on the fifth and lit up my life. Seeing the flower bouquet in his hands gave me the certainty that all would be fine. My concerns started dissipating, and there was no reason to fear the future.

"How have you felt?"

"Bad. But now that you're here, I feel much better."

"Forgive me. It isn't fair for you to carry all this weight alone, but everything happened too suddenly. I needed time to assimilate it."

"And what have you thought?"

"Listen, I know you're against abortion, but I did my research among my friends. In the navy there is this guy who went through the same situation recently, and he knows about a clinic where they can help us. The place is safe and clean, and they don't ask questions. I believe we would only have to go through that difficult moment, and later, when we're ready, we will plan a family."

I tried to talk but was impeded by a knot in my throat that felt like a golf ball. It asphyxiated me and didn't allow me to pronounce a word. I let the tears run down my cheek and took the courage to express my thoughts.

"I told you before, and I repeat it now. I'm 100% against abortion. I can't imagine how any mother could even think about it. Because now that I'm pregnant, I'm feeling something I never felt before. I sense that baby inside me and the great responsibility to protect and love it. I would be incapable of killing it."

"But you're not killing anyone. What you're carrying in your womb is not a baby— it's a fetus, and I'm sure it doesn't feel anything. It hasn't even developed."

"You can call our baby as you wish. I said what I think, and for now, it's best if you leave. I'm not feeling well, and I would like to rest."

"I don't want to leave you like this. To be clear, I don't want to leave you. I thought that might be a solution as we both are young to become parents, but if you are prepared, with more of a reason, I should be, since I'm older. As I said, we're in this together, and now, we're a family of three."

I threw myself in his arms as I listened to his words and cried for, I don't know how long. I tried to stop, but I couldn't hold back my tears. The pregnancy made me more emotional, and I didn't want that moment to end. Holding the father of my baby, I felt we were already a family. And my child, as any other, needed a father.

"What I said before shames me, Mariana. You're admirable. You will be the best mother."

"I don't know if I will succeed, but I'll try. And I'm certain we will have a beautiful baby who will make both of us proud."

"My mother's house is pretty big with enough land. On the upper part, we can build ours, and our little boy will have a patio and a spacious garden where he can play when he grows up."

"And if it's a girl?"

"Mariana, please, don't torture me, is our first. It will be a boy."

"We need to start thinking about a name."

"It's necessary to think about many things. In the meantime, let's start planning so that you move in with me as soon as the baby is born."

"In your mother's house? Do you think she will accept me?"

"Most likely, she won't. She doesn't like anyone. I must warn you she is a difficult person. None of my previous girlfriends had passed the test with her."

"And then?"

"Then, don't let that bother you. I'm not trying to discourage you. I only want you to be prepared."

"And if she doesn't react well regarding the pregnancy matter?"

"That would be her problem. You and I must concentrate on planning the house and preparing everything for the baby's birth. I've always liked construction, and my buddies can help me to build it. In the meantime, I will buy some things and store them in the warehouse. That way, when the time comes, the expenses won't be that big."

"I will speak with my mom tomorrow. She is now excited about a man she's dating, and I don't think she'll mind me leaving the house. I rarely see her anyway. She's not even aware of my pregnancy. But I'm still worried about your mother. What if she tries to separate us?"

"Don't say foolishness. I'm not a child to listen to my mom. For now, the priority is to take care of you and have a healthy baby. And when he's born, we'll live together. Once the hardest part is over, which will probably be the first two years, we'll start building the house, and in one more year, we will get married."

"Are you serious?"

"Don't you think everything we've been saying is serious?"

"Yes, but we hadn't talked about marriage before."

"That was before. Now, things have changed. Everything is happening fast in our lives. I've had many doubts, but when you were in the hospital, I thought I could've lost you forever. I knew that if something I was sure of was wanting to be with you, and if anything scared me, it was the fear of losing you."

NINETEEN

Katya

12 years later

"Thirteen more exams to grade, and I don't want to know anything about students, exams, or anything similar. I only want to get lost in the clouds, fall asleep and wake up in another continent with two of my favorite teachers and dearest friends."

"I don't want to know about students either. It seems unreal that the date finally arrived after a year of planning this trip. At last, this coming Monday, we will leave Denver to be in Barcelona the morning after. On second thought, with the time difference, we'll sleep on the plane and, after twelve hours, will arrive in the late afternoon, just in time to take advantage of our first night in Europe."

"How wonderful! This trip will be different from the one to Africa. Now there will be three of us, and the activities will be different, although I don't lose hope of going back to Africa, you know how I feel about animals, and I doubt that any trip could exceed the magnificent experience of being in contact with nature and the loving creatures of the animal kingdom."

"I know, Katya. But I hardly believe that animals, regardless of how much you love them, could take your mind away from Martin. I can't believe that you were about to marry him while that insensible man not only had a wife but a child with an incurable illness. What kind of man can abandon his family under those circumstances and, on top of everything, keep it hidden from you?"

"The kind that crosses my path. First, Zayed, and a few years later, this one. This is the second time that I involuntarily get involved with a married one, not to mention the weird ones. It's said that I attract them like honey to bees."

"Let's try our luck with the Europeans. I would love to meet a Swiss man. Besides being handsome, they happen to be good husbands."

"I would like to find one of the race *men*. I'm tired of the picturesque cases that always jump into my life."

"You'll see that this trip will be different. We have a lot to see, and thirty days will pass flying. Please call Letty and remind her not to be late. I don't want to imagine the tragedy if that woman loses the flight. I will do my part and call her this evening, and hopefully, this time, our reminders will help."

After a hassle-free flight, we arrived in Barcelona around 6 p.m. local time. We settled in our room, showered, and initiated our first Spanish night wandering in *Paseo Las Ramblas*.

At 9 p.m., there was still daylight. After eating the most exquisite tapas in a hole in the wall restaurant nearby, we were amazed that at 10 p.m., the sun began to set, and the locals started getting ready to party. Despite our tour leaving early the following morning, we didn't waste a moment and opted to experience Barcelona at night.

If someone likes women in this world, I must say the Spanish men, who always chased us regardless of where we were— on a tour, at a restaurant, at a store, and even at a museum. The chase started when we left our hotel.

Spain possesses a characteristic charm. We fell in love with Barcelona. We were impressed by the Prado Museum in Madrid and the lighted beach of San Sebastián. But among those, we thought Andalucía was the most beautiful— We visited Córdoba, Granada, and Sevilla, each one with an individual magnetism. Nevertheless, Granada has no comparison. La Alhambra and the Generalife Gardens, with their Medieval architecture of Moroccan influence, are perhaps the jewels of them all.

Moreover, the gypsy caves, with their flamenco show on a full-moon night, wrap the visitors in a spellbound that penetrates the skin layers.

On our first day in Europe in a foreign place, not only on another continent but because we started in Spain, it was a dramatic change that enticed us to know more, submerge ourselves in that unknown world, and the treasure of experiences awaiting us in each country.

From Spain, we flew to Paris, where we remained for five days, wishing we had many more dedicated to this vibrant place of incomparable beauty with so much to see, it is worth making a trip exclusively to Paris to appreciate it in full splendor. We were fortunate to stay at a hotel near the Eiffel Tower, and at night, from our room, we witnessed the breathtaking view of the illuminated tower.

We dedicated two days to the impressive museums of the Louvre and Orsay. On the city tour, we visited Les Champs Élysées, and L'Arc de Triomphe, among other landmarks. We saw the painters of Montmartre in action on our way to the Sacred Heart Basilica. Later, we embarked on a sunset Seine River Cruise to enjoy the unique romantic atmosphere of Paris. On our day at leisure, we satisfied our curiosity by seeing the world-renowned Lafayette Galleries and savored a delightful French dinner at a local restaurant. On our last day, we went to the Versailles Palace and parted with heartache for not having had the time to take an excursion to Champagne or many other places we would have wanted to see.

Our journey continued to Belgium, starting in Brussels, a city that welcomed us with the captivating glamour of the Grand-Place. Despite the dozens of adjectives to describe it, the best way is the place that would be unforgivable not to see, classified by the grandeur of its Gothic architecture as one of the world's most beautiful plazas.

Three days later, we were dazzled by the elegance of Brussels, its architecture, museums, and like most tourists, by the *Manneken Pis*— the city symbol.

After a delicious, freshly made waffle breakfast with Nutella, we boarded the bus to Brugge to witness the picturesque beauty and winding waterways of this iconic city. The intoxicating smell coming from the chocolate factories, the little Medieval cobbled streets, and its architectonic jewels make this town a fairy tale where time stops to store the memories in our minds for an eternity.

As we moved on with our trip, the days shortened. We went to bed late and started the tours early, always intending to sleep on the bus or train, but the alluring landscapes surrounding us prevented us from closing our eyes, not to miss an instant of what we could hardly see again once back home.

We crossed Luxembourg, where we spent the rest of the afternoon and night in the city to continue on route to Switzerland the following morning. Coming from the Colorado mountains, we thought we had seen everything, but is there a place in the world that can be compared to the Swiss Alps? Being Switzerland the penultimate country in our itinerary, we wanted to see it all— We only went to Zurich and Geneva. After taking the city tour in Zurich that included the main tourist attractions, we decided to take a day excursion to the Swiss Villages.

I mentioned before that we saw places of indescribable charm and the Swiss towns and villages we saw many years before in the movie Heidi, now that we were there, our fascination exceeded our aspirations' limit. Switzerland has everything—beautiful people, gorgeous landscapes, unique buildings, and, as an extra value for those like me addicted to chocolates, the chocolate factories.

Before entering Italy, the last country on our trip, we headed to Geneva where a visit to the United Nations Office ended our stay with a flourish. Had we had more time, we would've extended our days in this fascinating country.

Now, in Italy, we commenced in Venice and perceived the notorious difference between Switzerland and Italy despite being neighbors. Italians are more casual and, on the same token, more passionate, even with the street arguments on balconies from one building to another. That came to our attention, and we found it amusing. Later, we found out that they were not arguing. It was their expressive way of communicating.

Since Venice is surrounded by water, it makes a dramatic difference from the rest of the previous cities. Because Italy was the final spot on our trip and having such a busy itinerary ahead in Rome and Florence, in Venice, we only took a tour to Murano to see the blown glass pieces of art that originated there. The rest of the time, we spent leisurely people-watching and wine-sipping, feeding the pigeons at St. Mark's Square. We walked through the narrow ancient streets and hopped aboard the Vaporetto, or motorboat used for public transportation.

In the heart of the Tuscany region, Florence is the art reign regarding painting, sculpture, and the world-renowned Renaissance architecture, stunning from every angle. We visited a few galleries and had the privilege to see, among other Renaissance masterpieces, the original David from Michelangelo. As exhausted as we ended up after a long day of sightseeing tours, we didn't miss the opportunity of a night stroll through the Ponte Vecchio, a frequent habit among Florence locals and tourists.

In Rome, we booked a hotel a few feet from the Coliseum. With this perfect location, we got around tourist attractions on foot.

As the sun set in Plaza Navona, a typical Roman artists' spot, where musicians, mimes, acrobats, painters, and many more of the bohemian world concentrate, some selling their works and others delighting tourists with their presentations, usually with a hat, a jar, or any container to deposit donations at the end, we stopped for a moment, and listen to a violinist. The magic emitted from the strings of his violin hypnotized us for the time we took to finish the gelato we savored, fascinated by the artist's ability.

When depositing a euro at the end, the leather bracelet on the violinist caught my eye— it was the same as one I had bought in Guadalajara several years before.

"Where does your bracelet come from?" I asked him in English, not knowing the language he spoke. "I bought one like yours in Mexico a while ago."

"It's a long story." He replied.

By the sadness he reflected in his smile, I didn't want to ask more. I only deposited a Euro, and my friends and I walked to one of the restaurants by the Plaza.

After dinner, sipping a grappa, someone behind my back approached us at the table. "The lady with my twin bracelet." Said the violinist, asking if he could buy us an espresso.

"You're welcome to join us." I replied, "But don't feel obligated to invite us."

"What is it? Don't you think I make enough money to buy some pretty ladies a coffee? I wouldn't let myself be carried away by appearances."

During the conversation, he said he was Greek and lived in Athens from birth until he moved to Rome. Previously, he owned a marketing company and did well. But after the shocking loss of his long-time relationship girlfriend due to a traffic accident, he sold his house and his business and moved to Rome, undecided about what to do with the rest of his life. He also said that his girlfriend gave him that bracelet upon her return from a trip to Mexico, and he'd worn it since then. It was his lucky charm.

When I asked him if he did well playing the violin at the Plaza, he answered with doubtful thinking— "Not as well as I did before with my company, but enough to live a carefree life. I can make up to 250-300 euros daily in summertime."

"You're amazingly talented. You could be a famous concert artist."

"I'm not pursuing fame. I learned to play the violin as a child, and I love to do it. I have no pressure in my life. And if one day I don't feel like working, I don't have to."

Our sadness for leaving Italy appeared to grow worse on the last day of our trip. The Vatican visit and the spiritual connection with the unsurpassed beauty of works of art and architecture that this little country possesses added to an unmatched trip experience we would repeat at the first opportunity.

On my return, I brought in my luggage, a suitcase full of shopping, immense gratitude for the moments we lived, and nostalgia knowing that soon I would be about six thousand miles away from Jonas, the Greek violinist who won my heart in a few hours with his talent and humbleness.

TWENTY

Months went by, and Jonas and I kept in touch. He wrote me letters, and I anxiously waited for them, and on special occasions like Christmas, birthdays, and sometimes even on the not-so-special, we phoned each other. As time passed, the frequency of the letters diminished until the content of my mailbox was reduced to only promotions and unwanted mail.
I had my feet on the ground and knew that long-distance relationships hardly ever work. But I was still excited and had my hopes set on this relationship.

Busy with my work and routine, I moved on with my life, and three years later, two days before Easter, I received a phone call that unbalanced me. I was trying to have everything ready to host Sandy and her family. They would spend Easter with me, go to church together, and afterward to brunch as it had been a custom of mine since childhood.

"Hello, Katya, how are you?"

"Jonas? I didn't expect your call. We lost contact a while ago. Where are you?"

"I'm in Venice. The last time we spoke, I believe I still was in Rome. From there, I moved to Monte Carlo for a short period and came back to Rome. Now I live in Venice."

"Doing what?"

"Following my passion, playing the violin, except that I do it now at Saint Mark Plaza."

"And may I ask, what made you call me after all this time?"

"Well, I've been thinking it's time for a change— I want to go to America. You have told me about Denver, Colorado. And I believe that's the place I want to see."

"Are you coming on vacation? For how long?"

"Not exactly on vacation. I want to establish myself there. Are you still single?"

"I'm in the same situation that I was in on my trip to Europe, enjoying my life plentifully, and just to be clear, I'm not married."

"Do you have someone in your life?"

"I have many people in my life, and I feel fortunate about it."

"I'm referring to someone in particular, like a boyfriend or fiancée"

"Neither one nor the other. I believe I'm good that way. How about you? Are you still single?"

"That's why I'm calling you. How do you like the idea of living together? I think we are alike in many aspects. We can give it a try. And when you feel ready, we can travel through the United States. We can discover different places together. I don't need anything but my violin."

"And I need much more than a man playing the violin in public plazas. I'm sorry, Jonas, but I think this is a crazy idea. I wish you luck. And I suggest you don't change your residency. Perhaps here you won't make the same money you did in Rome the last time we spoke."

From that day on, I realized that marriage was not for me. Nonetheless, in the beginning, I would've liked to have my own family and raise children, I thought I had enough with my students. My responsibility toward them had always been as one of a second mother. And if I hadn't married before, it wasn't because of the lack of proposals but because a stable man had never been interested in me. I understood that my future was not next to one bohemian guy playing the violin or any other unorganized man like the ones that showed up in my life. What I was looking for in a man, more than anything else, was emotional and financial stability. However, the second one was not a must. I made enough money with my work to live a comfortable life, but it wasn't my intention either to despise a rich man who showed up in my place one day, willing to share his future with me.

I liked to live well and had the means to do it. I lived happily and never regretted what I didn't have. Rather appreciated the privileges I received— a family close to me, although we didn't live in the same city. My parents had passed, but I still had a close relationship with my brother and sister.

I had nephews and nieces that I adored as if they were my children, and I had childhood friends with whom, over the years, the friendship intensified. And my friend's children, since I saw them born and growing up, I also saw them as my own. NO! I didn't need to drag an unstable man to feel happy. Neither did I need a travel partner. I had close friends who were always willing to keep me company on my trips, regardless of the destination.

Ten Years later

It seems like now it's serious. This is the end of my career. Close to thirty years dedicated to teaching. How many generations of future lawyers, architects, doctors, engineers, and even teachers like me who will continue my work, although I would have liked to have exclusively home runs in my teaching career, despite my struggle and, against my will, some students got lost on the way without me being able to rescue them. The pain about the ones I couldn't lead to the right path will always be part of me— but each destiny is written, and it's not up to anyone but to ourselves to get out of situations that inevitably will lead us to a ravine if we don't take the right action at the precise moment.

For instants, I wavered for the people I would leave behind— Paco and Ana were some of them. I met Paco when I started working for the school. He was also a teacher who began four years before me.

"Welcome," he said on my first day with a warm smile that made me feel at home.

"I'm Francisco, but you can call me Paco. If one day you talk about me as Francisco, no one will know who you're referring to. I also like to joke. You will notice it with time, but I'm here to help you with whatever you need."

"Thank you. In the beginning, the help of my coworkers is what I will need the most."

"You look confident about yourself. Maybe you're the one who could help me at one point, but if you never require anything, at least allow me to give you one piece of advice that I'm pretty sure will be valuable throughout your career."

"And I'm anxious to receive it."

"You will face some hard times when you're in charge of teenage students, but don't allow them, not even for a minute, to think they can direct the orchestra. They are here to carry the instruments. And it must be clear to them from the beginning."

I was always grateful to Paco for that advice, not only for that, and for giving me a helping hand when I needed it but for his sincere friendship and for that Sunday when he invited me to a barbecue at his house to celebrate his wife's birthday. The same as Paco, Ana, his wife, became instantaneous friends.

Despite Paco's retirement four years before me, Ana, he, and I kept the bond created 30 years before.

Soon, I will be in another city under different circumstances. Mixed feelings take over me. On one side, that much needed change, and on the other, the sadness of leaving those behind who have been like my family for all these years. I will miss many of them, and the idea of retirement excites me, except that I'm not ready for it. At 54 years old, I feel that I have a long way to go and that there are many things in life that I still can do. After thinking about it for a year, Ana, who worked in real estate, convinced me to study to obtain my license as an agent.

"You have a whole world to discover," she said at the beginning of our conversations. "Many students aiming at the real estate agent career don't make it for two reasons— because there's a lot to study and they think they have too much to learn, or because of the competition. But these two won't be obstacles to you. Your personality will help you to succeed in this field, and as soon as you start selling, the more you sell, the bigger the satisfaction. Besides, who knows if you might meet your Robert Redford once you start selling millionaire mansions."

That's what convinced me to venture into this new career. The Robert Redford part was discharged the moment she mentioned it. Years ago, I accepted my fate as an independent woman. Then, I learned to enjoy it.

One week after I retired from teaching, I focused on my studies. I had planned a trip to the Caribbean, but that would have to stay on the back burner for some time. I wanted to obtain my license as soon as possible and was anxious to test myself on an activity up to then unknown to me.

It took me less than six months to finish my course and obtain my license without complications.

DOMINANCE DELUSIONS

During my last week in Denver, I spoke to Ana, leaving her in charge of my two rental properties — my house and one small condominium acquired a few years back as an investment and which had been rented since then.

I hired a moving truck to transport my furniture to a provisional warehouse in Las Vegas. I rented an apartment for a month in that city and dedicated myself to filling a small U-Haul trailer with essential things. I hooked it to my car to initiate my trip to Nevada, where a different life and a spring of experiences awaited me.

TWENTY-ONE

Mariana

At 20 weeks into the pregnancy, we decided on an ultrasound to find out the sex of our baby. Whatever the results were, I would be happy. I just asked life to allow me the complete happiness of bringing a baby radiant with health into this world. I would've loved to have a baby girl, but Carlos Alberto's discomfort was evident each time I brought up the possibility. He was clinging to a boy and concentrated all his emotions on that idea. My stress levels spiraled each time we talked about it. On the day of the ultrasound, despite having left the alcohol and drugs since my last time in the hospital, I wished I could have lost myself in the effects of alcohol or anything to help me control my fear.

The peace transmitted by the sonographer while doing the study prepared me for any outcome, but in that instant after the radiologist's interpretation when he told us— "You can start choosing a boy's name," it was like hearing a voice from heaven that made me float on clouds. That news allowed us to live our happiest moment since the beginning of the pregnancy.

Being pregnant, like countless other women in my state, I experienced self-doubt annoyance which added to my hyper sensibility. Carlos Alberto loved me. I had no doubt about it, but some men think that the word man is a synonym for macho, and being macho is not compatible with faithfulness— and on my twentieth week of pregnancy, he had abrupt personality changes, suddenly he was loving and later became aggressive, sometimes he insulted me and left the house, and some others, just left the house, to return late at night with a deep alcohol smell. The idea of him going back to the way he was at the beginning of our relationship and falling deeper into drugs, destroying what we, with love, had built, terrified me.

Frequently, his mood swings made me fall into depression, but I touched my belly and felt a light that invaded my whole being. I could spend hours talking to my baby. About my plans for our future, the immense happiness he would bring to our lives, and my desperation for the day to arrive when I finally would hold him in my arms. And amid those unidirectional conversations, I felt soft kicks, sometimes not that soft, that drew a gigantic smile on my face. I knew it was my baby answering because he was understanding. And at his level of a tiny little piece of the angel he was, he wanted to participate in those monologues.

His father continued with his unexpected personality changes. At one moment, he showed a bad mood, feeling that his casual youth would be soon interrupted by forced fatherhood, and later he had the same enthusiasm as me for the arrival of our future son. When he was on the ship, on his return, he stopped at the Navy store and came home loaded with baby clothes, toy ships, stuffed animals, and anything appealing to his eyes. But his great enthusiasm was about that tiny sailor outfit that our baby would have to wait at least six months to start wearing, but his dad was ready to put it on his son since the day of his birth.

I stopped working at the store two months after I found out I was pregnant and dedicated myself to working at home, cleaning, and cooking...Yes, cooking. Since I didn't know how to boil an egg before, I decided to take advantage of the free classes that Social Security offered. In addition to cooking, I studied home economics and prenatal care.

I was a few days away from Ricky's birth. We agreed to name him Carlos Ricardo, and from that instant, I started calling him Ricky, which is short for Ricardo. My pregnancy continued its regular course, but as any woman in my state, the last weeks, mostly the final days, felt endless. I was exhausted and uncomfortable, rather desperate to welcome my baby and that significant change that was about to happen in my life.

One afternoon, being alone at home and Carlos Alberto on the ship, I started to feel contractions, and the pain was driving me crazy. I couldn't imagine the intensity of that pain and how women could resist it, but wise nature gives us the necessary strength to overcome it before compensating us with the arrival of a child.

My mom was working, and I had no other option but to call one of Carlos Alberto's brothers. As I was advised before, every time we touched the subject. Unlike the previous occasions when the neighbors took me to the hospital, my future brother-in-law showed up in less than ten minutes in his latest model Ford Taurus. And since Tecate was such a small city, in even less than that, I was checking in the hospital.

Carlos Alberto's brother started making phone calls. And little by little, the visitors showed up. First, his mother and some members of his family, then my mother, and it was until the day after, when the baby was born, that gave plenty of time for his dad to be present.

I remember the labor pains, and I find it impossible to have been able to bear them. But once my baby was born and I held him in my arms, I don't have words to describe that feeling. It looked like a miracle that such a tiny thing could've come out of my body. Happiness overflew within me. It was superior to me. And now, when I think about those unbearable pains, I would suffer them again with a smile, knowing the enormous satisfaction that followed those moments.

I loved my little boy from the instant I saw him born. I adored him before when we communicated with each other. He brought peace to my life in my harsh times. His dad was also crazy for him, and he felt proud of that little person, so tender and helpless with that need for protection that brightened our world with his presence. Not only Carlos Alberto but his mother and his whole family felt a deep love for Ricky. My mom was also delighted with her grandson and didn't waste a minute she could spend with him.

After he was born, we moved to my soon-to-be mother-in-law's house. Her lack of sympathy toward me was evident, but her desire to be close to Ricky made her presence just about tolerable when she was around, especially on those days when Carlos Alberto was not at home.

As much as I tried to accept her, it was crystal clear that she disliked me. Upset by the economic status difference, she committed to assigning me the heaviest cleaning chores in the house's common areas, such as the patio and the garden, and, when Carlos Alberto was in San Diego, she made me cut the grass with that burdensome old machine that even her son hated to use.

In the beginning, I asked myself if things would've been different if I had had some professional degree, or if I had come from a wealthy family, but soon, I discarded that idea when I realized that none of her children wanted to live with her. Her husband had left her a couple of years before to move in with another woman. Her neighbors tried to avoid her, and her circle of friends narrowed down to only one, whom my mother-in-law consistently criticized and vice versa. In conclusion, if I wanted to find an adjective to describe her – *a difficult person* – it would be the most suitable.

At five p.m. on a Friday afternoon, Carlos Alberto's mobile phone rang while I was feeding Ricky. After a few seconds of puzzled silence, by his agitated tone of voice, I understood something wrong had happened. Submerged in my responsibility and unable to speed up my baby's feeding process, my anxiety began to expand as the questioning on Carlos Alberto's side continued. His expressions of wonder and disbelief anguished me until hanging up, he could inform me about the tragic event we wish we would've never found out about.

"Carlos Alberto, who were you talking to? What happened?"

"Something horrible, Mariana. I don't know how to tell you this because I know how much it will affect you."

"For God's sake, man, you're scaring me. Tell me whatever you have to say."

"Is the baby asleep? Put him in the crib, and I'll tell you everything."

"Ricky is asleep. Now, can you tell me what happened?"

"Do you remember Esteban? He was in the car with us the night we met."

"Yes. I remember we met afterward on different occasions, and soon after, he separated from our group. What happened to him?"

"He separated from our group then because his girlfriend was pregnant, and from all of us, he was the first to get married. But since the start, it was he who introduced us to drugs. He was much deeper than any of us."

"And?"

"He had a fatal accident. The car he was driving with his wife and child overturned. They all fell into a deep ravine. They said the three of them died instantly. The saddest thing is that all of this could have been avoided. It seems it was intentional."

"What do you mean by intentional?"

"The brakes on the pickup truck failed, which is inconceivable since it was new. It just came out of the agency. It's still unclear who's responsible for orchestrating the accident for Esteban. It was not the intention to end with the family. Every time they went out together, they drove the wife's SUV. It's odd that on this occasion, they were in the pickup. An unfortunate accident!"

"Like it could happen to us, to our little angel who's not guilty of anything. I don't want this. I don't accept it."

Mariana, please control yourself. Stop crying already. Something like this would never happen to us."

"How could you be sure?"

"I am. Because I don't deal drugs and I don't get in trouble. Please calm down and trust me. You won't be a widow, at least not for this reason. You're not in danger either, let alone Ricky. You know the two of you mean the world to me, and I would never put you at risk, especially Ricky, who, as you said, is a little angel without any guilt."

TWENTY-TWO

A few days later, at Esteban's funeral, I saw my friends Malú, Selena, and Rosita after a long time of not seeing them. Malú looked bad. She resembled a ghost consumed by drugs. Her overdone makeup could not hide the bruises and beatings caused by Cesar. My heart broke to see her like that. With deep sorrow, I realized that despite being alive, life had also ended for her.

On the flip side, seeing Rosita brought me back some optimism. We talked for a prolonged time. Holding each other, we mutually consoled, grateful for our friendship and trying to eliminate the pain caused by the injustice of life.

"I need your help," she said. And her unexpected comment disconcerted me. "I don't want to continue like this," she added. "I don't want to end up like Esteban, and as for Malú and Selena, you and I know her days are numbered."

"Are you still with Raymundo?"

"No. We broke up a few months ago. At first, he made my life miserable. But I believe I was lucky. He already found someone else, and thanks to that, he left me alone."

"And you're still doing drugs?"

"Getting out is not easy. But I don't do it as frequently as before. I wish I could be clean. And that's why I need your help. How did you do it? Where did you get the strength?"

"I think my case was unusual because I managed to get out at the beginning. A little after my suicide attempt. I received several signs. Above all, seeing so many good people around who cared about me pushed me to my decision. In your case, you have your family. They love you, and I'm sure they would be willing to do whatever it takes to help you. The question here is, what are you willing to do?"

"I don't doubt they will help me. But I don't trust myself to do it alone— I need a rehab center. The problem is that I don't know where to find it or how to start searching."

"On that, I can help. At the church where I go, there is this guy who helps in the sacristy and works at the priests' house cleaning and taking care of the chores needed there, and as a second job, he works at an orphanage two days a week. It seems like everyone at church likes him. I always see that they take him food and give him extra work here and there, but the most admirable thing is that he comes from a rehab center and has been clean for six years. All I know is that the center is in Tijuana, and people say it's good. I'll ask him about it. And as soon as I know something, I'll keep you in the loop."

"You don't know how much I appreciate it. The idea of ending up as Malú or Selena terrifies me. But that's not it— I feel guilty for not being there for my brother in his last months before passing. Because of my stupidity and false escape, I could not be with him, and he's not here anymore to forgive me. Hopefully, my parents will someday."

Over time, Esteban's tragedy was left behind. Rosita joined a rehab center. I didn't see her for some time, but I knew from her family that things were on the right path.

I was clinging to the immense happiness that Ricky brought to our lives. Despite Carlos Alberto adoring his son, he continued with his moody temper, and his behavior hurt me. He hastily left with his friends and came home late at night with a strong smell of alcohol. I had no peace of mind seeing him walking the tightrope and thinking he would return to the drugs at any moment.

Not long after, those little escapades became more frequent, and the smell of alcohol blended with traces of women's perfume or lipstick and makeup spots. Ricky was only seven months old, and some nights I spent alone carrying my insecurity, my humiliation, and my rage to know that while I was at home dealing with my mother-in-law's bad temper and offenses, her son went out to have fun with other women as if I didn't exist.

We kept on that swing of emotions— suddenly, he was the loving father and a perfect husband, and not long after, he got tired, and the change occurred. The only thing that kept us together was Ricky's joy in our lives and the family we were proud to be by having a child like him. Our baby began to take his first steps. And I spent my time following him around. He was restless, and I feared he would fall or hurt himself. I made my everyday life a permanent duty to watch over my baby, to ensure nothing bad happened to him.

Time passed surprisingly quickly. Without being aware, we were already planning Ricky's birthday party. Because it was his first year, Carlos Alberto and his mother wanted to spend money as if there were no tomorrow. On my side, the only guest was my mom, but they, on the other side, had an endless family list. Part of that family I'd had the opportunity to meet before. But on the day of the party, I knew the rest.

Besides his brothers, he had several aunts, cousins, nephews, and nieces. He didn't mind the frivolous spending, organizing his son's party that he was too young to remember in the future. However, we, his parents, were proud of having done everything to see him happy, running around and playing at his first birthday party.

DOMINANCE DELUSIONS

We hired a taco truck, a hot dog cart, and a Popsicle cart. There were different games and an unnecessary variety of prizes. We were surrounded by balloons and children's decorations throughout the garden. Ricky received an outrageous quantity of presents on his aunts' side that seemed to compete in bringing the most.

Our little boy had more energy than ever before, more than his parents and all the guests together. He ended up with sticky hands from the cake and traces of cake and dirt from the forehead to his shorts, legs, and everything his little body could've absorbed.

In the end, all the adults in the house were exhausted, but the memory of having done the impossible to give our son a happy day on the celebration of his first birthday was priceless.

After a while, we initiated the construction of the house, or rather, the apartment, and the economic pressure began with the construction. Carlos Alberto's savings vanished like the smoke flowing out the crack of a window. Meaningless arguments frequently arose. Above all, every time we had to buy materials or pay one of the occasionally hired workers. But for the most part, fights emerged due to that responsibility that none of us planned and happened in such a sudden way that came to transform our lives.

We fought and later made up. And that was the best part of the ups and downs in our relationship. It excited the two of us to see the progress in the apartment, which, despite being small and on the second floor, was independent, with our kitchen, bathroom, and private entrance, which meant our privacy. We directed full attention to the functional aspect, and because everything was new, it caused a well-being sensation. We were not planning luxury. We only wanted a roof to live under, but something we gave priority to perfection was our baby's room.

I used to spend hours looking at home decor magazines and made several trips to the furniture and paint stores, looking for bathroom furniture and everything required in a new house. We chose blue to paint Ricky's room with children's designs in different colors. It was the first room finished, with astonishing results, and as we advanced on the construction of our small place, my happiness grew. Being Carlos Alberto so busy with his work, I was dedicated to the furnishing and decoration of our place, and that didn't bother me— it was a positive distraction and a good excuse to escape, at least momentarily, from my mother-in-law's abundant and constant mistreats.

Once our apartment was finished, and we were ready to move, I couldn't have felt more satisfied. I loved it. It was the first place I could consider mine and everything to my taste. I felt happy, and the reason, besides everything was modern and new, with each detail planned to the extreme, was knowing that I wouldn't have to run into Carlos Alberto's mother each time I had to use the kitchen, or the bathroom or any other area of the house and having to put up with her hints that after she had too much to drink, turned into insults.

Once settled in our place, the next step was our wedding. I've never had a passport before. I didn't see the need either, but Carlos Alberto was a US citizen and wanted me to apply for residency as soon as we were married. He wanted me, among other things, to go to San Diego and see the Naval Base where he worked. And at the same time, to have the benefit of shopping at the Navy store.

As we carried on with our plans to marry in a couple of months, the frequent fights continued. They were caused mainly by his unfaithfulness. I was seventeen years old and didn't have the intelligence to handle a man's cheating situation. A young woman, except in rare cases, is immature, and that means being jealous. It hurt me to know that my future husband was seeing other women. His violent behavior, at times, bothered me, and it scared me to realize he was doing drugs again. He started slowly by smoking marijuana, and far from diminishing his use, it was visibly increasing, the same way that increased the severity of the drugs used with which, little by little, he felt more comfortable.

TWENTY-THREE

Our wedding plans continued, and now, I ask myself why I did it. It is for the same reason that we humans, inexplicably, make mistakes. I was young and in love. I thought that once married, our love would grow. Like seeds we water and care for them from the beginning to see their fruits. But when a relationship is damaged, the reality is different.

When Ricky turned three, Carlos Alberto and I decided to legalize our situation. We were a family, established in our own home, with a son we adored. And if we had gone through storms, still inside, there was a common ground— the flame that at the beginning brought us together continued alive, and together, we wanted to see our child grow up and that he always felt protected by his parents.

At that time, I would've liked a religious ceremony. But we had our plan and wanted to stick to it. The first step was the legal wedding to facilitate the process of my residency in the United States. Once I obtained my permit, we would marry in San Diego to continue with the procedure, which included Ricky, who, according to his father, should've been born in the

USA. Every time the opportunity arose, he rubbed on my face to have been pregnant without a passport and that his child was denied the right to be born in the USA as his father did.

Unlike previous parties for Ricky's birthdays, the wedding was simple. It was only to comply with the legal marriage requirement, which did not include a celebration. After a private ceremony in Tecate, we had a late lunch at El Rodeo, a steak house in Tijuana. The restaurant was a little dark to my taste, but the food was exquisite, with unsurpassed service. It was an intimate wedding. The only guests were his mother and mine, his brothers, and a few close friends. The group didn't exceed 20 people.

Coming back home, I felt like a princess in my little castle. My apartment was far from extraordinary, but I loved it. It was modern and functional. I wouldn't describe it as a luxury place, but didn't lack anything. And despite my Papa Jimmy always doing the impossible to give us the best to the extent of his abilities, I hadn't lived before in a place like that. I spent hours contemplating what my husband and I had accomplished. And what we had built being together with our child was the best gift life could've given us.

Regrettably, it took my happiness to disappear, the same time a cloud casually crossing our path takes to vanish. We passed the initial phase of the romance. The arguments, fights, and insults became frequent. We crossed the line of respect, and everything started to fall apart because once a couple loses respect for each other, there's nothing left to be rescued.

Among the nightmares of our past mistakes that make us reflect on our lives and the direction we follow, amid desperation, I opened my eyes to the worst mistake in my life— my marriage. The first stains, despite my effort to clean them so as not to leave traces, were already part of our relationship. Thinking that with time, things change is a false hope because they do change not to improve but to intensify the human being's defects and to make deeper those intolerable details that damage the closeness in a couple.

Carlos Alberto wanted to start the legal petition for Ricky and me. He wished to live in San Diego, and I had no preference for one city or the other. But it was an opportunity to establish some distance from his mother, who disapproved of our relationship since the beginning and knew how to increase the flame to lead us to separation over time. She strategically didn't object to our marriage, knowing it was condemned to failure before becoming official.

My husband continued drinking and doing drugs. Although he adored his son, perhaps the responsibility of knowing there was no turning back to what before was a relationship with no other ties than our own will, now he increased his unfaithfulness, which to me, since I still loved him, was unbearable. During those periods of abandonment, when I had to deal with his mother's offenses and her negative influence on her son, a bridge with a weak foundation that was impossible to cross originated in our marriage.

I didn't speak English then, and my husband, although Mexican, dominated the language. However, his Spanish needed much improvement. We frequently joked, and I made fun of his accent. If I understand now how wrong it is to make fun of people's flaws, I saw it as funny back then. Later, I learned that it only takes a few drinks, and those small actions are the missing logs to ignite the fire, and fights, disrespect, and abuse arise.

If many times before, I had been insulted and degraded, a day arrived when I decided that things had gone too far. I couldn't bear to be lowered to such a degree because I didn't know how much more a drunk or drug-crazed man could do.

One night, changing my clothes, getting ready to go to bed, seeing Carlos Alberto drunk, and listening to the nonsense he was saying in Spanish, I made the biggest mistake I could've done— I made fun of him and opened the box of worms. In a fit of rage and not caring that I was in my underwear, he yelled at me and beat me, ordering me to leave his house, for he had built it, and I had nothing to do there. Not finding anything wiser to do, I ignored him, which increased his ire and resulted in a more intense beating. He dragged me outside the house, kicking and leaving me half-dressed on the sidewalk with my mouth bleeding, one purple eye, and my heart oppressed by humiliation.

In the face of such commotion, the neighbors came to help me. I wanted to run and take refuge at my mom's house, but I could not leave my child abandoned in the hands of the monster his father had turned. Swallowing my pride, I spent the night at the neighbors' house. The lady lent me a robe so as not to cause more fuss among the men in the family, and I had to wait until sunrise to look for a solution for my life and my son's.

The sleepless nights were familiar. There were some when I could only fall asleep for two or, at the most, three hours. But, on this occasion, in between sobs, I counted every minute of each endless hour—I tried to calm down and think about Ricky, who was my reason to continue living. The exits through the false door were left behind some while ago. Now, I had someone to live for, someone who deserved a better life than the one I had lived, and that, gave me the strength to overcome any obstacle in my way.

Drenched in tears and asphyxiated by sobs, I wondered when I failed. If I did not doubt that limitless love had existed at the beginning of that erroneous relationship, when did it start to deviate, and how was it possible to have been so blind not to see the whirlpool that was pulling me more each time in the wrong direction?

I looked for answers that didn't come to my mind, but the endurance that made me stay on my feet since the first abuse I was a victim of helped me to detour my thoughts, concentrating on the hope of tomorrow, on the humongous happiness that Ricky brought to my life. That happiness was mine. And no one could take it away from me. The merry moments I have lived with my child were a small example of everything yet to come. That was my redemption. If it was God's will to make me a mother at the age of sixteen, it was to accelerate the happy moments and infinite satisfaction that my son would bring me.

Waiting for the sunrise, the hours seemed eternal. I was desperate to get my things out of the house to move in with my mom, but not without taking my child. I feared Carlos Alberto's reaction when I told him I was taking our son, but I knew that sometimes, crazed by alcohol or drugs, he went to the extreme with his actions and later repented because he was not a mean person. He had an explosive temper, which was the cause of his biggest mistakes, but in times of reflection and when consumed by a feeling of guilt, occasionally, he opened the door for a dialogue.

It was hard to convince him, but he finally understood that a temporary separation was needed to heal our wounds and give each other time to decide which path we wanted to follow for our future.

I realized the pain it caused him to separate from his son. But he knew I needed my time and my space. He was working, and his mother was not the fit person to take care of our son. Above all, it was unhealthy for the child to be alone without supervision with someone like his grandmother, who used to drink at the same level and with the same frequency as her son.

Knowing that divorce was inevitable at 19 years old scared me, but the weight leaned toward the extraordinary peaceful feeling of being with my mom again. Although we never had that mother-daughter closeness that I would've liked, this time, circumstances were different as it was her attitude. I don't know if it was due to Ricky's presence, but our relationship became more cordial. Besides, she had health issues and felt happy to have us by her side.

For the first time since Ricky's birth, I decided to go back to work. I needed the income while my situation was legalized. In the meantime, his father built castles in the air, imagining we would be together again, but the distance between us was greater each time.

"The store is closed now. They will return soon." Said a gentleman while I waited outside a skateboard shop where I went to apply for a job.

"The sign says they will be back in fifteen minutes, but I've been waiting longer, and they are not here yet."

"They shouldn't take long. Are you here about the job?"

"Yes. You too?"

"No." He answered with a smile that confused me at the beginning. "I'm the owner of the business across the street. From there, I saw you waiting and wanted to tell you that sometimes they go to the bank and close for a few minutes, but they won't take long. They urgently need an employee. By the way, I'm Gilberto. And you?"

"I'm Mariana. Nice to meet you, sir."

Respectfully, I extended my hand and felt a vigorous handshake accompanied by a comment that made me blush.

"Nice to meet you, Mariana. But please, don't call me sir. If we're going to be neighbors, you can call me Gilberto. I'm almost positive they will hire you. Although, you seem too young to work. Is this your first time working?"

"I started my first job at nine years old."

"Well, that was unexpected. But Luis will interview you. Luis is the name of the owner. In the meantime, I must return to work, or my secretary will fire me. I hope to see you later. Good luck."

TWENTY-FOUR

"I apologize for the delay. I went to the bank, and there were more people than usual. Have you been waiting long?"

"It doesn't matter. I'm here about the job."

"You're too young to work. May I ask how old?"

"Nineteen."

"Do you have experience in sales or skateboards? These are the main items we sell here."

"I don't have any experience, but I can assure you, I learn quickly. Please, sir, I'm in great need of work."

"Come, follow me to the office to fill out an application, and you will tell me why the urgency."

Without going into details, I had to tell him I was separated and had a child. Everything in the interview seemed to run smoothly until I mentioned my son. I noticed a sudden change in his attitude.

"You seem intelligent and responsible. I believe you when you say you can learn quickly, but I'll be honest. From what you told me, you just separated and have a child. Suppose I hire you, and suddenly you decide to go back to your husband, and he doesn't want you to work. But also, you have a child, and children always require unexpected care. I wouldn't like you to start missing work because something happened at the last minute."

"I assure you that won't be the case. I'm decided. I will divorce. And as for my child, my mom can take care of him while I work."

"Look. This is what I propose. Tonight, before I close, I scheduled another interview. Let me analyze the two applications carefully, and I will call you. If I decide to hire you, when could you start?"

"I can come whenever you need me. If you wish, I could be here tomorrow morning before you open the shop."

Despite having felt confident during the interview, in the end, I left disappointed, thinking he wouldn't hire me. If I lost that opportunity, perhaps the same would happen in any other job once I exposed my situation. But things happen for a reason— having met the neighbor gave me a hint that he could influence his friend's decision, and I don't know why I thought that. I just hoped I wasn't wrong.

That night, I spent it next to the phone, hoping to hear it ring. Sadly, it didn't. I thought that the morning after, I would get the paper to start looking for other options. Early in the morning, I fed Ricky and bathed him, and before ten, my heart jumped at the same time I jumped from my chair when I heard the phone ring.

"Good morning. Is this Mariana?"

"This is she."

"Hi. This is Luis Robledo, the owner of the skateboard shop. I was analyzing your application, and I'm considering giving you an opportunity. I would like you to start tomorrow. Could you come this afternoon so I can give you some instructions and teach you a few things?"

"Of course. What time is convenient for you?"

"Between 5 and 6, whenever you can."

"At 5.15 that afternoon, I was at the shop. Mr. Robledo briefly instructed me about his merchandise, and by 6 p.m., I was free to go home. I was hired, and that skyrocketed my self-confidence. Gilberto was outside his mobile home business. He crossed the street as he saw me leaving and asked me how it went. I answered, "From this day on, we will be neighbors because I'm hired."

We talked for about 30 minutes. He seemed a kind person. Our talk was everything but personal. We lost track of time until suddenly, I put my feet on the ground and remembered my obligations. I rushed to say goodbye, so I could be on time to take care of Ricky.

My week went by smoothly. I was learning quickly. And the satisfaction of being productive, combined with the internal peace I hadn't experienced in a long time, made me feel like a new person. Gilberto showed up every day at the shop at different times, and when there were no customers, we had conversations for long periods. Soon, I realized I was getting used to it.

When the weekend arrived, and I took Ricky to his father, I looked for an appropriate moment to tell him about my job. I didn't want him to give me a hard time or find the minimum excuse to stop me from working, but before I expected, he had already been drinking, and I thought the wisest thing was to keep quiet for a few days. I was positive he would disapprove of my decision, and I didn't want to take any risks.

The following week was no different from the previous. Gilberto continued visiting the shop. Through his daily visits, I started discovering some details of his life. He was 20 years older than me. He was 39 then, and the two of us were separated from our spouses, going through that purgatory when problems corner two people sometime ago in love to make the drastic separation decision. The only difference in our situation was that he had initiated the divorce process. Occasionally, when there were no customers in the store, it was only Gilberto and I, and when my boss was around, he also took part in the conversation since he and Gilberto had a close relationship of several years.

Soon, the three of us teamed up. Sometimes, we ordered food and ate at the shop, and occasionally, in the mornings, Gilberto brought coffee and doughnuts or arrived before we opened, and I brewed fresh coffee.

I learned my job quickly and discovered that I was good at sales. I liked to keep the shop clean and everything in order. My boss was pleased with my performance.

Doing my job in a peaceful atmosphere where I felt motivated represented a self-esteem overcoat— not realizing it before, I was getting used to mistreatment and humiliation, and the fights were a daily fare. In this new life where I was starting to raise my head to the surface to exhale, I suddenly felt, they were sinking me, trying to drown me again.

I intended to hide the job issue from Carlos Alberto, but after three weeks, I decided it was best for him to know. Sooner or later, he would find out, and the more I let time pass, the worse the consequences for me would be. My job came up in our conversation because he thought we would reunite soon. When I told him I needed more time and, for the time being, I was well with my life. He was enraged with one of his used fits of anger.

Since that argument, he decided that Ricky shouldn't be with my mom all the time— his week would be divided into equal parts between his mother and mine. That destabilized my serenity, which I was getting used to, more each day.

The first message of disagreement was to send his mother to the shop since he was working. The woman had accumulated rage, not because I had left the house and his son, but because I brought Ricky with me and she adored him. It was he who brought meaning to their lives. Seeing me at the shop with that motivation and self-sufficiency that I hadn't experienced in a long time, and that encouraged me every morning to get up and to look and feel good, and to see my performance at work, provoked her rage, and not caring about my boss's presence, she started cursing and took it out on me as she used to.

My boss saw himself forced to intervene to get her out of the store, telling her that whatever she had to say, she had to do it in private and in the privacy of her house or mine, not at the shop. And, if her intentions were not to buy anything, she wasn't welcome there.

That scene embarrassed me. Luckily, Gilberto wasn't there at that time. But I was sure it wouldn't take long to find out with great detail about that incident. I tried to avoid him— first, because of the embarrassment, and second, I didn't know when Carlos Alberto's mother could come back and see me talking to Gilberto would exceed the limit of her patience, and who knows what she was capable of.

The scandals continued. Often, the woman showed up in the evenings after her long, lonely happy hours at home and when she had lost the little common sense she might have had. Sometimes, she did it when my boss was there, and he stopped her in the blink of an eye. But on occasions, I was alone, and I felt a knot in my stomach when I saw her entering the shop— and some other times, she did it when there were customers around. Each time, my fear grew, thinking that my boss would lose his patience and would end up letting me go to avoid future scenes.

For a while, I had to continue going through that unpleasant situation until the day when Carlos Alberto showed up. That was the final straw. To my bad luck, Gilberto and I were talking outside the store. He barely had time to say goodbye and cross the street toward his business. As soon as Carlos Alberto parked his car, he entered and stormed in, insulting me with the lowest language of his repertoire, pulling me by the hair and pushing me, and uncontrollably throwing the sportswear and some other merchandise on the floor. He held my arms as tight as he did when we were alone, leaving bruises that, regardless of how hard I tried to ignore them, the softest touch of my clothes made me remember them— his yelling could be heard not only at Gilberto's business but at the other businesses on the block. Before I realized it, Gilberto and two other neighbors were in the store, telling Carlos Alberto to leave immediately before the police arrived.

Carlos Alberto didn't intimidate easily, but he knew that because of his work, the first thing to avoid was a public scandal, especially when the police had to intervene.

If there was any reason to prolong the beginning of my divorce, with the shows performed by Carlos Alberto and his mother, what they accomplished by joining forces to embarrass me was to push me to initiate the process. Gilberto referred his lawyer to me, and since then, Ricky's father became one more chapter of my shameful story. The only thing that helped me to leave behind all the offenses and abuse I was a victim of was the respect and patience that Gilberto treated me with and the security he made me feel being with him.

TWENTY-FIVE

Katya

Every three hours, we took turns driving, stopping to stretch our legs, drink a refreshing beverage, check the tires, and make sure the tank had plenty of gas. I decided to make the trip alone, and one day before I left, Paco showed up at my place without a previous call.

"So now, this is final. I see you have everything packed. You always have been organized and independent, but I think this time, I won't let you make that trip of almost 800 miles alone. What if you feel bad on the road or something happens to you? A woman shouldn't do that by herself."

"Some time ago, I think we left behind that distinction between a man and a woman. If a man can do it, so can I, since I don't have a man by my side. Besides, I have been to Africa, feeding the giraffes from my window, where I closely experienced the zebra migration. And I had wild animals at a short distance from our vehicle. I have traveled all over the world, and in many circumstances, I have been alone, and I know how to overcome danger. Don't think I'm intimidated by a possible auto mishap."

"Yes, Katya, but you're not 30 years old anymore. Look, I talked to Ana. It's been a while since we've been to Las Vegas, and there are several new hotels that we would like to see, and you know she likes to play roulette, so it is decided— I'll go with you and help you, at least on the first day, to settle down. I'm renting a hotel room close to your apartment. And the day after, we collect Ana from the airport. We'll look for one of the new hotels on the strip. You said that your plans for the first week were to get to know Las Vegas, and the three of us could do it together. I don't see why we couldn't say goodbye with a fun vacation."

"You do lots of crazy things, Paco. But I admit this is not one of them. I'm going to take your word. After all, I think that to Ana, as to you and me, this little distraction will do us good."

The first week was entirely a vacation. Paco, Ana, and I were dedicated to seeing the nocturnal side of Vegas— that vibrant city where people never sleep, where the lights blend with dawn, nights are endless, and daytime doesn't exist. One night, we saw the MGM show, and another night, the one from Liberace, one as impressive as the other, different but with the same squandering of talent, luxury, and extravagance. In the mornings, we had the homework of finding the best hotel buffets. Each of us had a favorite, but we enjoyed them all the same.

I took advantage of Ana's expertise during her stay to look for a promising residential area for business. And that's where I decided to establish myself.

"Las Vegas is a developing city," she said, "you must focus on the workforce. All the hotels and the tourist industry grow thanks to the Mexicans and Latinos who fulfill the work of waiters, maids, and all the cleaning areas that people in this country dislike— but Latinos come to make money. And as soon as they make it, they buy their first property and start building an inheritance for their children."

"And how can we find out where these people live?"

"That will be your job. At night, go out to have a drink at the different hotel bars and take some coins for the machines. Eventually, the employees will show up and ask if you need anything. Engage in conversations with them, and once you detect the areas, look for properties and focus on those."

"But here, there won't be those extravagant houses all we agents dream about selling."

"No. Here, you won't find the glamour of those houses, but you'll start taking your first bold steps. Once you establish your client portfolio, you will be surprised at how loyal your buyers can be. And if they're happy with you, they will buy their first affordable home, and later, they will refer you to their relatives, friends, and coworkers. After some time, they will decide to buy a larger house, and that's how the chain starts."

"You don't know how grateful I am to you for making this trip with me and for your valuable advice, which will get me started."

"Just allow me to tell you one last thing. Don't be carried away by temptation. And don't leave this area where you will find your little goldmine. Rent an apartment for six months. And as soon as you see the opportunity, buy a house as an investment that you will later sell to buy a better one. Once you have your first property, consider making a party and invite contractors, pool service professionals, tile setters, and painters, among others. Although, at first, they won't send you buyers, you offer to send them yours. Over time, you will see the fruit of your labor. You're in the precise city. And you can make it big."

I stuck to the original plan. In less than two years, I already had a modest client portfolio. I bought a house in an area where I enjoyed it, without being the house I fantasized about.

Because I lived in a city where people who were not addicted were still attracted to gambling, I frequently received company from out of town. It was either one friend or the other, and my job was to find out about the latest shows, which was the most attractive part to my family and friends.

After five years, doubts rattled in my head about how much longer I could stand living in Las Vegas. Excess also tires. A place saturated with action attracts people born in the middle of the action, and I realized I didn't fit in that group.

One evening at an international dance competition, I woke up to the call of a hobby, which I'd longed for quite some time. Looking at those women with their long chiffon dresses, dancing gracefully through the entire room with their couples, gave me the impression that they had contact with each other's bodies for aesthetic reasons. It seemed as if they flew over clouds following the melodies' rhythm without the need to be held. Their only contact was the meeting of glances with the mystery of hiding an act of intimacy. I knew I wanted to be part of that dancers' group, whose only concern was perfect coordination following the music's direction.

That week, I dedicated myself to finding a dance academy for beginners like me. Although I didn't have a partner, they informed me that I shouldn't be concerned about it since there were others in my situation, and the teacher always offered his help to those who were starting.

Casually, at a bar happy hour, I met Pierre. Talking to him about my dancing lessons, he told me about a restaurant where couples have dinner, and there's an adjacent room where they play live music from Thursday to Sunday. They switch from disco music to tango, salsa, and others. On Thursdays, they play ballroom music, and people display their artistic skills as they would at a competition. "If you want, one of these nights, we can go," he said. "You will love it. It's exciting."

I'm unsure if it was the following Thursday or any other that came after that, but Pierre and I developed a friendship like I haven't done for a while with anyone else. We went out to dinner, dancing, concerts, buffets, and anything else we felt attracted to. Pierre was 18 years younger than me, and surprisingly, despite the age difference, we shared the same taste for everything, men included, because the only thing he did not like were women.

With time, we became inseparable. In the ballroom, being a professional dancer, he surpassed me outrageously. The day I met him, he'd recently finished a contract with one of the largest hotels in Las Vegas. In the meantime, they called him temporarily for several shows, and he was trying to start a choreography company for private events.

I kept working and dancing, and after a year, I saw the opportunity to participate in my first senior competition. Competing with people my approximate age gave me confidence, and I was excited about my progress. But sometimes, life pulls us in a different direction when we plan a special event. I didn't know how or why, but one day, during a routine exploration by my gynecologist, she discovered cancer in my right breast.

Since she detected it at its early stage, there was no reason for concern, but enough to suspend some plans— among them, my first competition. The initial step was surgery to remove the tumor and make sure to get rid of it completely. The oncologist suggested radiation after surgery. He authorized me to dance while my body could resist it at the beginning of treatments, but he insisted on me being careful and focused, above all, on fighting that disease.

At first, I felt upset, thinking I didn't do anything to deserve that. But my friends and coworkers convinced me that an illness doesn't develop because we deserve it— it just appears for no reason, and going through it gives us the strength to get out of unexpected circumstances. I'd always faced life with a positive attitude, but being realistic, I'm not Saint Theresa. I'm human, and occasionally, I fall into rage and despair.

There are support groups, and Pierre convinced me to participate in one. Going through the discomfort that radiation causes, there were days when I thought the sun didn't shine in my world and, perhaps, I would never see it shine again, but I soon found out that breast cancer is more common than we women think and that I was lucky to have detected it before it metastasized because once it starts spreading to other parts of the body, it is almost impossible or much more difficult to fight it.

TWENTY-SIX

Upon receiving the package containing my 4000-dollar dress, I desperately opened the box to try the dress on, hoping the alterations would have come perfectly, according to the initial try. It was a splendid blue gown. I'm not sure if it was for 4000, but buying it at a specialty store in Las Vegas for costumes and show business attires was the best I could get. I felt like a celebrity, opening that rectangular gray box with a waxed finish packed with such excellence, and containing the most expensive dress I'd acquired until then. It filled all the requirements. I had visualized that gown for a few years. Above all, I was mesmerized by that circular skirt of several yards of chiffon that would move around the whole room with each of my movements.

After trying it on, I imagined it was specially designed for me. It fit me like a glove. Although I couldn't stop thinking about the 4000 dollars, it didn't bother me either. It was my first competition, and the previous year I had to postpone it due to my illness. Now that the cancer was in remission and I felt well in all aspects, I saw no reason to scrimp on something so important to me.

Having my dress ready, I still had to go shopping to choose the accessories and shoes and confirm the appointment with the makeup artist, hair stylist, and nail specialist. It was a National competition that would be televised by one of the most reputable TV stations in the United States.

Since I was in a category of people 60 years and older, Pierre couldn't be my dancing partner, but the one they assigned me at the academy and I made a perfect couple, and both of us had only one goal in mind— to win a medal finalizing in the first three places.

On the day of the competition, one of my nieces, her husband, and a group of coworkers from the real estate office were present. I don't consider myself a nervous person. But that night, for the first time, I felt dominated by nervousness, listening to the speaker when they mentioned the names of my dancing partner and mine. I took a deep breath before starting, and for three minutes, my mind got lost in the music. The thunderous applause at the end brought me back to reality, sure to have reached the desired point close to perfection.

I almost fainted at the award ceremony when I received the silver medal. A celebration followed, and the party did not end until late at night. I don't recall having felt tired or the need to leave early. The attendants, mostly, were the ones starting to say their goodbyes. By the end, the only ones left were my niece with her husband, and Pierre, who would've wanted to stay until they started serving the breakfast buffet.

After that competition which was the only thing keeping me in Vegas, I discovered an academy in San Diego where I could continue my lessons and participate in the annual contests. A while ago, while searching for the ideal place to change my residency, La Jolla popped up at the top of the list. I felt ready for semi-retirement, working half-time in the real estate business and, on the other hand, doing the volunteer work that I'd wanted for so long. My passion for animals grew each time, and since San Diego had such superior conservation work to support wildlife, it was the ideal place for a weekend volunteer job.

I started making plans for my relocation, and when I told Pierre about my decision, he proposed to move in with me.

"I always wanted to live in La Jolla," he said, "but I believe what was missing was someone to help me make that decision. At first, while you and I find a house, we can share one. I'll help you with the expenses, and we hang out at the beaches, restaurants, and everything there is to know in San Diego, especially in the La Jolla area."

"I don't know, Pierre. I'm very used to my independence. You and I are good friends. And if this doesn't work, I wouldn't like to risk our friendship."

"Don't say foolishness. Why wouldn't it work? We are alike in everything. If you want, you set the rules. I follow orders, my general." Putting his extended hand on his forehead, barely touching the edge with his index finger, he concluded with a military salute.

"Give me some time to think about it, but first, in case I agree, these are my rules— we will share rent and monthly expenses, and we'll also go for equal shares on food and cleaning items. And talking about it, you know I'm a clean-and-order freak. I don't want to see unmade beds or dirty cups or glasses. And your momentary boyfriends, you take to a hotel because I don't want them in the house. If you agree, maybe we can try for the first months."

"Agreed. Perhaps there, I can start my dancing school or continue with choreographies as I do here, but if I decide to do that, I want to grow in that field. I would love to dedicate myself exclusively to corporate events or millionaire weddings. How exciting! Why haven't we thought about it before?" Clapping his hands, Pierre was agitated like a child imagining his future in La Jolla, California.

"Now that I see you so excited, I guess I couldn't refuse. Start making the necessary arrangements to leave in two months."

"Katya, what's the first thing we'll do arriving in San Diego?"

"The first thing will be to locate the house I rented, drop the suitcases, and then we'll go to the hotel I reserved for two nights in case the moving company will delay and won't arrive the day after."

"Perfect. And after we settle in the hotel, what shall we do?"

"The hotel is located in an area called Old Town with lots of restaurants, the majority Mexican, but the two of us like Mexican food, and a margarita to relax would do us good, and at the same time, we eat."

"And after that, can we go to downtown San Diego?"

"Of course not. The farthest I will get tonight is the bed in my room, and I hope to sleep for at least 12 hours."

"Oh Katya, don't be a party pooper. Look, I've been asking around— all the action is in downtown San Diego. It's dotted with restaurants and bars and places with music. That's at the top of my list. However, I'm also dying to see La Jolla, but they say that's a daytime activity around its beaches. At night, the town is dead. Please, please, I beg you, let's visit downtown tonight."

"Did you say tonight?"

"Yes. I'm also dying to go to Little Italy and Hillcrest. They say they are so much fun but those are in opposite directions. The real spot is in the heart of downtown between 5th and 4th street."

"Oh, Pierre, your eyes are bigger than your brain. After a six-hour drive and everything left to do in San Diego, do you think we will feel like partying tonight?"

"I'm always in a party mood, and so are you. Where that I'm tired bull@%*% is coming from?" You never feel tired."

"Never under different circumstances, but when people travel, they get tired, especially after all that hustle and bustle awaiting us."

"There will be plenty of time to relax. You said the first week was to get acquainted with the city and to settle down. And that you had no intentions of working until the following week."

"That's what I said, but you're acting as if we came on vacation for two days— it seems you haven't realized that we're going to live there, and we'll have plenty of time to go out and party."

"But tonight, we have to go out and celebrate."

"Enough already, Pierre! You're driving me crazy. Let's get there first, and then we'll figure out what we feel like doing."

The city and Las Vegas desert got lost several hours before. The road sign that read 11 miles to San Diego led us to that new world we were about to discover. Following the map, we located the Clairemont area, three miles from La Jolla. Continuing through Governor Drive, we arrived at the residential area where I rented the house— a property built at the beginning of the '80s, mostly remodeled with a spacious kitchen, two bedrooms, and a small studio. The backyard with orange, lemon, and pomegranate trees, promised enjoyable, relaxing afternoons with a fragrant breeze unique to the enviable San Diego climate.

"Look, Pierre, we have a grocery store close to the house. It is one of those that specializes in healthy foods. It even sells vitamins and supplements. It's always convenient to have one close."

"Fantastic. Stop there to get a bottle of wine."

"Why don't we arrive at the house first? Then we will check in at the hotel. And then, we go out to dinner. There, we don't need to drive. The restaurants are within walking distance. And afterward, we worry about the bottle of wine."

With a disappointed frown, and as a rare case, Pierre decided that the best was not to insist and wait to see how things developed.

"There's the hotel, Pierre. It's not a four-star, but it is picturesque and well-located. Let's get our suitcases. We settle down in our rooms and go out to eat. What do you feel like?"

"Food. I'm starving."

"That makes two of us. And you'll have to forgive me, but I can't assure you I won't fall asleep on the table after a margarita. I'm exhausted."

"Maybe you were right. I'm also tired."

"What do you think about that restaurant in the corner? It looks like fewer people are waiting to get in."

"I prefer the one across the street where the mariachi is playing. I think that's the spot."

"I prefer the first where we can get a table. And if you wish, you can later bring me a serenade with the mariachi."

"As the colonel, Mrs. Katya says."

"At least we agree on something, but let's split. I'll walk toward the restaurant in the corner and ask what the waiting time is, and you do the same where the mariachi is playing. And we'll eat at the one with a shorter wait time."

Two margaritas and three tacos were enough to conclude our first night in San Diego. I wish I had a crystal ball to know what fate awaited me in that city with a partner that, in the previous years, I couldn't get to know completely until we shared the same roof.

TWENTY-SEVEN

Mariana

Four years living with Gilberto have shown me a different side of life. I always asked myself what made my mom move in with Papa Jimmy, who was 29 years older than her. She didn't give the impression of being in love, seeing other men all the time, and hoping to find her prince charming one day. I'm unaware of the situation that led them to live together. But I'm convinced their circumstances were different from Gilberto's and mine.

Despite him being 20 years older than me, I believe it was that chemistry from the day I met him, and to see the kind way he talked to me, his intelligence, and his respect toward me. And, of course, the physical attraction— all those factors make me think we will be together till the end of our days. And together, we will see our family grow.

Now that I think, after so many stormy days in my life I'm, enjoying seeing the sun come out at last. And if I hadn't had to go through that seesaw with Carlos Alberto regarding Ricky's custody and for hurting me immensely, opposing for all that time to divorce me, I would have lived a complete happiness as the one I began experiencing when he met Socorro, his girlfriend. Although she also contributed with her grain of sand to make my life impossible, I must be grateful because thanks to her, they were together, and that made me a free woman to start a new life by Gilberto's side.

My relationship with him was in its fourth year, and the idea had been swirling in our heads for quite some time. We wanted to give Ricky a brother or a sister, someone he could play with. Notwithstanding, Gilberto accepted my son and saw him as his own from the beginning— he also embraced the thought of us having a child together.

Things started to change. The happy memories of Ricky's childhood slowly fade away. His once docile and gentle temper suddenly turned into rebelliousness and indifference. Sometimes, he even crossed the line of aggression. My world was turning upside down. I had gone through tortuous moments in my life, but the pain of feeling I was losing my child was intolerable.

Sharing custody of my son with his father only increased my moments of uneasiness. Each time Ricky returned from spending a weekend with his dad, the situation in our home became unbearable.

Things gradually continued escalating until one day, I was stunned after a senseless argument that raised a red flag, and I knew I had to act fast.

"Ricky, it is two o'clock in the afternoon, and look at the mess in your room. You can't leave clothes all over the floor. This room was neat and clean before you came."

"Leave me alone and stop bothering me already."

"Don't talk to me like that. I'm your mother."

"For now."

"Hold your horses, young boy. I gave birth to you. And I sacrificed everything for you since you were born, but…wait a minute! What did you mean, for now?"

"Well, you know my dad's girlfriend, Socorro. She's super cool, and my dad says the three of us are moving to Washington, and I won't have to come with you anymore. All you do is scold me."

"Where did the Washington thing come from? Your father hasn't mentioned anything to me about it."

"They will transfer him on his work, and I want to go with them. Neither my dad nor Socorro scold me, and they even let me drink with them if I want to."

"Did you say drink? Did your father lose his mind? You're a brat. You're seven years old. At your age, children go to school and obey their parents. They don't drink."

"My dad says I'm not supposed to act like a little girl. I must learn to drink like real men do."

"That was the only thing missing! This man lost the little grain of sanity he had left in him. I feel like not letting you go back to his house."

"Stop annoying me. I'm calling my dad, and I will tell him to come and pick me up. Socorro is right when she says you're bitter and that she, my dad, and I will have a good time away from you."

I was about to slap him when Ricky intercepted my hand in the air. We argued and tussled. And in a fit of hysteria, I exploded into tears because of my limitations and because I realized how far we've come. At that moment, I knew I had to act immediately. The clock was ticking.

As Gilberto arrived home, he found me in a sea of tears, with a tiredness impossible to overcome. The same exhaustion with which I usually ended up after a long session of tears. Ricky could sense my suffering, and by then, he was calm and with a different attitude, but I couldn't forget his words drilling my ears— the thought of losing him ate me alive.

"Mariana, what's going on? Why are you like this?" Gilberto asked upon entering our room.

"I'm losing him, Gilberto. And I feel desperate."

"Are you referring to Ricky? You know he adores you. How can you say you're losing him? You two have been inseparable since his birth."

"We had been until the day that woman appeared in Carlos Alberto's life. Since then, my problems with Ricky began. I know she's turning him against me, and now, I just found out that Carlos Alberto is being transferred to Washington, and he's considering taking my son with him. I can't let that happen."

"He can't do that. The two of you have shared custody. He can't take the child with him."

"You know he's capable of anything. And if that happens, I will go mad."

"I won't allow it. And I have the solution."

"Which is?"

"If your ex-husband wants to play dirty, so can we. In the same way he wants to take Ricky to Washington without your consent, we can take him to Ensenada without his. For a while, we've been talking about moving there. In my business, I've always had good customers from Ensenada. We move, taking Ricky with us, and Carlos Alberto won't know where we are."

"Don't you think that's too risky?"

"It's a risk we must take. Taking the child without his father's consent is considered kidnapping, and perhaps you will take a chance of losing custody. But in the Navy, when they deploy someone, they don't ask for their opinion— they only give the order. And it can vary, but sometimes, they only give them 30 days for their arrangements, and knowing Carlos Alberto, I don't think he would start opening an investigation if he couldn't follow up on it."

"Then, how much time do you think we could have before

he leaves if that's the case?"

"That, I don't know, but I don't think it will be this week. We have some days before you return Ricky to his father. Tomorrow, I will go to Ensenada to see if we can still live in the place we had planned and to address a few things regarding my business. I will call you from there to update you on the details. But before that, I want to ask you. Are you sure this is what you want to do?"

"100%. You don't need to study or be intelligent. A mother knows how to recognize the heart signals. I don't want to lose my son, and I feel I'm starting to lose him. I'm willing to do whatever it takes to avoid it."

"Well, things happen for a reason— how long have I been insisting on us moving to Ensenada? I believe this is what we needed to make the final decision and live a quiet life there."

"We have only five days. On Friday, Ricky needs to go back to his father. Do you think it will be enough time to do everything needed?"

"Stay calm, Mariana. I will try to return early from Ensenada, and then I will throw myself into finding out when Carlos Alberto needs to be in Washington."

"And how on earth are you going to do that?"

"Easily. I will ask Anselmo, who also works for the Navy. He'd been keeping me posted on all the stupidities Carlos Alberto does— you know he's not a saint of Anselmo's devotion."

After that talk with my husband, I calmed down and took advantage of the days Ricky had left with me to show him the immensity of my love, and if for someone I cared about above all in this world, it was him, and I was willing to do everything to make him happy.

The day after, early in the morning, I told Ricky we would go to the arcade games so he would play, and if he felt like it, I could also play with him. I exchanged a 20-dollar bill for coins to be sure he would have plenty to play all, or at least most of the games. And, while the machines sucked up my coins like a vacuum, the game was over after a couple of minutes, and it was time to refill the coins. Ricky was having a blast, as I'd never seen him before. He was thrilled— laughing and yelling each time he won. I tried to keep up, considering the limitations that a twelve-week pregnancy caused me.

After a fun morning, I took Ricky to eat tacos de adobada, which he would like to eat daily if he could. I don't know if it was a good decision regarding my wallet, since after so much released energy, he was so hungry, I thought he wouldn't stop ordering tacos, but I didn't regret either the tiredness or the expenses, as the reward exceeded the above when Ricky told me it had been a while since he had so much fun, and that he would've liked Gilberto to join us that day.

That was the desired moment, and I paused to initiate that talk with him.

"I was delighted as well, my love. You know how much I love you, and I feel bad when we argue. Yesterday, I perceived your aggressiveness. Is there something that Gilberto or I had done to make you feel bad?"

"No. You two always treat me right. And I have a good time when it's my turn to be with you."

"And is it true that you're better spending time with Socorro? Because yesterday you said that she's very cool, and you prefer to be with her."

"No, Mom. I want to be with you, but Socorro is constantly telling me that when I grow a little older, you and Gilberto will kick me out of the house, and since you're pregnant, as soon as the baby is born, you won't care about me anymore and you will abandon me as a dog, and I don't want that to happen."

"My love, that will never happen. Please, don't listen to Socorro. You know she's always drinking and talking nonsense. Even if I have one or three more babies, you will always have a special place in this house. You are a part of me because you and I are like a puzzle, and if a piece is missing, it's not complete— you're that piece, and no matter how many years pass, I will always need you because, without you, I could never be complete."

"Thank you, Mom. I wish I could stay with you and not have to go back to my dad. I also love him, but he's always drinking. That's the first thing they do when Socorro arrives. They both love to drink. And my dad, on occasions, frightens me. Sometimes his eyes look weird, his sight is strange, and that scares me."

"Has he really given you beer or something to drink while you're with him?"

"Yes, I only drink it because I don't want him to think that I'm little girl, but I don't like the taste. But on the other flip, I have to learn to be a man, like my dad says."

"Sometimes, we, parents, also make mistakes, Ricky. Don't listen to everything your dad says— a man is not a real man because of the amount of alcohol he drinks. Education is what makes a true man, his integrity, moral values, and the respect he has toward others, above all, women, children, and older people. Those are real men. And when the time comes, you will become one of them."

"I think so. That's what I want to be."

"And, with time, you will be. But tell me something else. Has your dad given you something besides beer?"

"Something other than beer? Like what?"

"I don't know, something different that you hadn't had before— something that makes you feel weird and makes your eyes look strange. Like your dad occasionally has them."

"No. They always lock themselves inside the room after they drink, and when they open the door, the room smells ugly, like something burnt. And sometimes it doesn't smell bad, but when they open the door, the two of them have the strangest look in their eyes."

"Ricky, don't you ever smoke. When your dad gives you anything to smoke or something unknown, tell him you have a headache and don't want to do it. Tell him to leave it for another day, but don't drink alcohol either, you're still young for it, and alcohol, especially at your age, doesn't lead to anything good. It will only destroy you."

TWENTY-EIGHT

"Mariana, how did it go with Ricky?"

"Better than the last time. I think it was an excellent idea to have taken him to the arcade, and at the end, I took him to eat tacos de adobada. You should've seen the transformation."

"Is he asleep?"

"Yes. I think he ended up tired."

"Perfect. That way, you and I can talk. I found the ideal house for us. We will leave tomorrow evening. I will leave the two of you settled in Ensenada and return to take our things as soon as possible. Between the pickup truck of my compadre Lalo and one of my trailers, we will take, if not all, most of the things."

"You think we'll have enough time?"

"By the time Carlos Alberto comes in four days, this house will be empty, and he'll have no clue where we will be."

"I know that man. He won't stop until he finds us."

"He will come on Friday evening to take Ricky with him, and if he doesn't find us, he won't do a thing because it will be late on the evening, and there's not much he can do over the weekend, and on Monday he will have to go back to work."

"The good thing is that being on the ship, he won't be able to do anything. He will remain there for a few days. That will help us to buy some time while I continue working on Ricky until I have him on my side. The only problem that I see is my mom's weak health. Besides, she will be the first one Carlos Alberto will contact, and when he doesn't find us, I'm afraid he will turn aggressive and hurt her. On the other hand, I must tell my mom where to find us."

"Don't worry about it. Your mom will come with us. As you said, her health is fragile. We can't leave her like that. And above all, we can't leave her now that she has changed so much and for the first time you are enjoying that mother-and-daughter relationship you longed for so many years."

Nightmares woke me up in the middle of the night. I didn't remember having had uninterrupted eight-hour sleep since the first day we moved to Ensenada. I saw Carlos Alberto showing up any minute, and I couldn't avoid the anguish of him ripping Ricky from my arms to take him away, who knows where, and I saw my child crying, not wanting to separate from me. The sweat running down my forehead blended in my cheeks with my tears, and I woke up running to his room to kiss his forehead and convince myself he was safe with me and no one, not even his father, could tear us apart.

= = = = =

From the beginning of my relationship with Gilberto, I gradually started to recuperate my peace. I didn't imagine I would end up living in Ensenada. And if my mom hadn't been so sick in her last months before passing, perhaps she would've remained living in Tecate, and I, with my frequent visits, trying to avoid unnecessary encounters with Ricky's father. I was grateful to Gilberto for taking my mom to spend her last days with us. And when she died, I felt blessed to have Gilberto by my side. He gave me the needed peace and strength, and with him in my life, I didn't fear facing Carlos Alberto when the time came.

The plan to take Ricky with us worked wonderfully, but only for a while. The day they knocked at the door, and when I opened and saw Carlos Alberto with his lawyer, I felt my legs give way, and the horrified expression on my face showed my adversary that regardless of my well-planned strategy, he was winning the battle.

"Hello, Mariana. Aren't you glad to see me?"

"How did you find me?"

"What a lack of courtesy of yours. Not even How are you? Nor, We missed you. But I'm not impolite like you. So, I will answer your question— I knew about your mom's death. Forgive me. I would've wanted to express my condolences before, but you left without saying goodbye, and I didn't know your whereabouts. It wasn't until a few weeks later when my dear mother-in-law turned stiff when, through your divorce lawyer, she could give me the address that showed on the death certificate."

"My lawyer gave you my address?"

"Yes. It's funny how things are— like the players of a certain team, they play for one and then switch to another. That's life! But, where's my son?"

"Please, don't take him away. I beg you. You're going to affect our child. Let's talk about it between you and me. We can reach an agreement. I know I acted in a moment of weakness without thinking. Forgive me. I promise you this won't happen again. You can set your rules now, but please, please, you and I, let's agree."

"Let's see. Let me have my lawyer explain that we don't have much time. You know I'm not good with words, but my lawyer here is a person of studies. He can make you understand the deal in this little game of yours."

"Look, lady. You had your son kidnapped for some time. It is not our intention to affect you, but if you don't want to end up in jail, the smartest thing you can do is deliver the boy to his dad on good terms. My client is the father and has the same right as you regarding the child custody."

In the face of a horror scene dominated by rage and frustration, I saw how they took my child, and I felt as if they had torn one part of my body. As if they were torturing me with electric shocks, debilitating my strength and will. I hugged him with my whole being, telling him we would see each other soon, and by doing that, I felt invaded by self-rejection, not positive if I was telling the truth.

= = = = =

"Tonight, Ignacio and I will discuss the last details, but before, I want to ask you for the last time. Are you sure about this?"

"Totally. I have no doubts. I have no other alternative."

"I agree with you. There's no other alternative. But you must think about the consequences because if something goes wrong, there's no turning back— that record will stay on you forever, in any country you live."

"I know, and yet I want to think positively. I want to imagine everything will be all right."

The morning after, we ate early, something light according to the plan. At 1:00 p.m., Ignacio showed up and asked me if I was ready, and after that, he and Gilberto talked about the last details.

Ignacio was Gilberto's close friend, and he trusted him as a brother. They've been inseparable since high school, and, when we spoke about my problems with Carlos Alberto, about my fear of not seeing Ricky again if his father took him to Washington with him, as his intentions were, Ignacio suggested he could help me cross the border illegally. He was not a smuggler but had a motorcycle business for off-road races.

Along with a group of friends, they participated each year in a race between Ensenada and La Paz, known as Baja 1000. The adrenaline rushing through the competitors' veins made them search for high-risk, inhospitable terrain. And, sometimes, he and his friends rode through dirt roads, defying the border patrol stations just for the fun of practicing on dangerous routes.

"Ignacio, you know I adore Mariana, and she's carrying our baby daughter in her womb. Please don't allow anything bad to happen." With a desperate plea, Gilberto told his friend, hoping to obtain that assurance that only fate could grant.

"Gilberto, you and I are like brothers. We have been together through good and bad times, and we've had it hard, but I'm sure that before you know it, this will be an occasion to celebrate. Besides, I also see Mariana as part of my family. I promise you to take care of her as I would with one of my sisters."

Ready to depart, I used the restroom for the last time. My braided hair was approximately eight inches below the shoulder. I wore dark beige sweatpants. The suggestion was to wear anything in earth tones. And it was the closest I found. I also wore my best pair of Nike tennis shoes. My favorite ones. I would've wanted to wear some older ones, but being those the most comfortable, they were my best option.

Among my belongings, I took only a small cross body bag that Gilberto got me at a sports store and a bottle of water with a maximum capacity of 16 ounces. I didn't have any ID or a mobile phone with me. On my left wrist, I wore a large face watch. In the hidden zippered bags of my sweatshirt, I kept my medal of San Francis of Assisi, some tissues, four one-dollar bills, and two other bills, one of 20 and one of 10, distributed between the left and right hidden bags.

Gilberto took Ignacio and me to drop us on the Mexican side of Tecate, to initiate our route. I noticed a small tear in one of his eyes— trying to hide it, he got close to me, kissed me, and said, "I'll see you later, on the other side. Don't worry about anything. Everything will be all right." We hugged, and it seemed he didn't want to let go of me. Although I didn't want to either, my anxiety about starting that trip to the unknown and arriving at my destination gave me the strength to continue.

We walked for an hour and a half. And during that time, Ignacio repeated his instructions every twenty minutes. And although I had memorized them, he didn't seem confident that I would follow them to the T. Suddenly, we stopped, and he said— "We are already in the United States. In twenty more minutes, we will arrive at the spot where Gilberto will pick you up. Once we are there, I must return, but please, I want to remind you what I have been telling you."

"Thank you, Ignacio, but I'll be all right. I don't see any border patrol around here."

"Not now, but they come out even from below the earth, and when you least expect them. You can't let your guard down or get distracted because even when you don't see them, there's a possibility that they might be watching you."

"I won't get distracted. I promise."

"That's what I wanted to hear. Now, it is close to three o'clock in the afternoon. The weather is starting to change. And by four, you will feel cold."

"I hope Gilberto won't have any setbacks and will be here on time."

"And I hope so, but I want to be sure you will follow my instructions— in the case that something happens, and Gilberto doesn't show up, don't stay waiting for him— go down to the road and ask for help, someone will help you, even the ones from the border patrol. The important thing is to avoid staying here all night. You have no idea how much the temperature can go down, and you could die from hypothermia."

We continued our journey until we found some rocks marked with three small, barely noticeable circles that someone had painted before. Upon approaching them, we stopped. And for the first time, I realized how cold the weather was turning in a matter of minutes. Ignacio took his jacket off and gave it to me.

"I must go." He said, "But before, I want you to tell me again what's the most important thing you will do."

"If the night falls and Gilberto hasn't come, I walk to the road and ask for help. This is no place for me to spend the night."

"Look, do you see straight down that black road? That leads to the freeway. It's not far from here. But don't wait till it gets dark because you might get lost. Gilberto won't take long. Everything will be all right."

That said, he hugged me. And I saw him drop out of sight.

At times, I felt anxious, but the baby I carried in my womb kept me company. She gave me strength and hope, and I talked to her the same way I did with Ricky during my harsh times, and that, caused me indescribable peace. Being in that situation, I convinced myself that I should overcome any obstacle because the end justifies the means, and the idea of soon reuniting with Ricky and that my baby girl could be born without any mishap and the thought of the family we would become soon, filled me with enthusiasm and, there was no place for fear.

Submerged in my thoughts while I patiently waited, I saw a patrol car getting close. I was sweating uncontrollably despite the afternoon feeling significantly colder. The K9 dog got off the patrol first, and I heard him barking close to me. Because of my poor knowledge, I didn't know much about the role of a canine working for the border patrol, and I felt fear. But not fear of being detected but of the dog biting my womb and hurting my child. Invaded by that cumulus of ignorance, I reminded behind the boulder, curled up in a fetal position, trying to protect my stomach to avoid a bite. In one or two seconds, I heard the agent and his K9 heading back to their patrol and rushing to the highest part of the hill to join other patrol cars.

Approximately five minutes later, in the distance, I distinguished a man approaching my direction— as he got closer, it worried me to see Ignacio instead of Gilberto.

"Get on the ground," he said, "and don't move. They stopped Gilberto up there. La migra caught him, and they are questioning him. If you turn your head up in the direction to your left, you can see the commotion with all those patrols up there."

I felt like I had a rude awakening with ice water on my face. I was letting my unborn girl and my son Ricky down. I exploded, asphyxiated by tears. And before I could articulate a word, Ignacio said there was no reason to worry.

"They are inspecting his car and will question him for a while, but they won't do anything to him. He's a US citizen with a clean record. They will let him go once they see they can't find anything. I only wanted to tell you not to anguish since it will take him longer than expected, but don't worry. As soon as they set him free, he'll come for you. Now I must go. Good luck!"

After saying that, he headed toward the road and disappeared in five minutes. If I permitted fear to dominate me, I would lose the battle, so I decided to wait patiently. In less than half an hour, Gilberto showed up. I threw myself into his arms, and he took me by the hand, saying there was no time to waste, to get immediately in the pickup truck and get down until reaching the road.

I followed his instructions. And none of us said a word until he broke the silence by saying— "You can sit down now, fasten your seat belt, and place Chacho on your legs. We succeeded in

75% of the plan. Now the only step missing is the final one. And it might be the decisive one. When we arrive at the checkpoint, we act naturally. And let me do the talking, as we agreed. But, in case they address you, repeat to me what you will say."

When I started talking, he interrupted me, advising me to take a deep breath. He said I was going in circles and had to get straight to the point. When the officer approached, if they asked me anything, I was to answer only.

The plan was to say we took our dog Chacho for a ride—that Gilberto took the wrong exit, and we got lost. I didn't have an ID because we were not going anywhere. We only took our dog searching for a place to walk.

We were three miles away from the checkpoint. And, if I had been relaxed all that time, convinced that everything would be fine, I started to fall apart at that moment. My heart was about to explode, and I feared they could listen to my heartbeat and I would ruin the plan.

As the crucial moment arrived, we held each other's hands and started laughing and crying hysterically.

"What happened?" I asked, not knowing what had just happened.

"A miracle," Gilberto answered. "Through all these years I've lived in Tecate, and with the hundreds of times I passed by this inspection point, it never, for once, this place has been closed."

"Why did they close it?"

"That, I don't know, but I have no interest in finding out—Welcome to the United States."

TWENTY-NINE

Katya

"Pierre, will you give me your part of the rent as we agreed? You're two months behind. I think you're failing to comply with your part of the agreement, and I told you before we moved to San Diego. I don't want this to affect our friendship."

"I don't want that either. Our friendship will last a lifetime, but I haven't found a place to start my business. I don't have the same income as you. If you are a little patient with me, I assure you that sooner than you expect, I will surprise you and catch up with all my debts."

"Of course, I'm patient with you, but I already showed you three places to initiate your business, and you don't like any."

"It's not that I don't like them, but none of them yells at me— this is the place. I must find the perfect one. That's something that your heart whispers to you. When you find what you're looking for, you feel the excitement and butterflies in your stomach, and up to now, I haven't felt it with any of the places I've seen."

"OOOKAY"

In my third month in San Diego, I sold my first house. I thought things would be easier, but the competition in this city was brutal, and I was unknown in this field. However, I didn't see a reason to disappoint me. I was not intimidated by the competitors. Luckily, I received my retirement. Besides, I had the income from my house in Las Vegas plus my other two properties in Denver. I had enough money to pay cash for a condominium in La Jolla and extra money to live for about a year without worries, even without sales. But that was going to the extreme— the hard part was to begin, and I already had my first sale. I was motivated.

Pierre was the one who worried me. I didn't see in him the personality to succeed or the drive to start a business. I didn't think he liked having a boss, either. I was hoping to be wrong and that soon he would find a financial solution to his future. He was a good friend, and I wanted to think we would continue traveling and going to theaters, concerts, and everything we used to do before.

It excited me to have found the area in La Jolla where I wanted to live. I only needed to find the precise moment to jump in when a property yelled at me— buy me. And I had a feeling it would happen soon. Every day, I received more listings. I knew I shouldn't rush, and it is true that when we find the right place, our heart is the one that lets us know.

"PIEEERRE."

"Heaven's sake, Katya, you make me nervous. What kind of yelling is that?"

"What kind of yelling? The kind from desperate Katya. It is three o'clock in the afternoon, and you haven't made your bed. You haven't even washed your dishes from breakfast. What is the matter with you?"

"Forgive me, forgive me, Katita. The thing is that I went shopping very early. My friend Maurice will pick me up later.

We're going to dinner. Let me show you the shirt I bought, it's awesome."

"Don't Katita me and leave your room and the kitchen clean before you leave. Who's Maurice?"

"He's a friend I met at the gym. Wait till you meet him. You're going to love him. He's super cool."

"I'm glad you met Maurice, but don't make me repeat this. Leave everything clean before you leave. Oh! I almost forgot the most important thing. I've been searching for dance academies and found the one I've been looking for. It's close by, and the instructor has won several competitions. He has so many students that he rejected some because he urgently needs an aide. He wants to find another teacher. Give me a minute, and I'll get his info."

"I appreciate it, but I'm not sure that's what I want to do. I come from Las Vegas, and the last thing I had in mind was to be an assistant to a dance instructor."

"You could take this job while you find what you're looking for. There's nothing wrong with having a steady income, and you will be dancing, which is what you like to do."

"Yes. But there are different forms of expressing one's art."

"And while you find a way to express your art, will you continue owing me the rent money?"

"I just paid you one month."

"And you still owe me one more. And another is coming in a few days."

"Listen, I will catch up soon, all right? I promise you."

"One more signature, Katya, and we're done. As a real estate agent, you might agree with me. This is an excellent buy."

"Yes. I was chasing this property for a while. Although it needs some updating, I was counting on that, and I'm happy I could acquire it. This had been my idea of the perfect place in the right location since I came to La Jolla for the first time."

"Congratulations, then. I'm pretty sure you will be happy living here."

"Pierre, let's have dinner in downtown San Diego. You choose. Let's celebrate."

"And the reason?"

"My new property. I placed an offer for a condominium in La Jolla, which was approved. It's the one I wanted. The area is safe, and the location is perfect— close to the mall, restaurants, and movie theaters. Besides, I was talking to the neighbors from the upper floor. They seem like decent people. That's essential if you want to live peacefully."

"Fabulous news. When shall we move?"

"We? Sounds to me, like many people, the agreement between you and me was to live together for the first months while I bought a house, and you decided what to do."

"But up to now, I haven't found a job."

"Because you don't want to. I gave you the information about the academy, and you didn't want to apply. But that doesn't matter now. As a friend and as a human being, you're one of a kind. But as a roommate, you're impossible. Working on the condo might take me at least two months before moving in. That will give you plenty of time to find a place to live. We will continue being friends but never again living under the same roof."

Once I settled down, I decided to replace Pierre with a couple of cats to keep me company. I went to the nearest pet adoption center, and I chose my two babies, identical, gray, short hair, British race— a boy and a girl, and I named them Louis and Louise. What helped me to distinguish them, in the beginning, was a white birthmark on the upper part of Louis' neck. The two were loving and tender, although Louise had a crankier temper.

I hoped they would keep me company for the rest of my days. It made me happy to see them when I got home.

My life had a balance then, and I felt nothing was missing. If my sales didn't move as fast as I would've liked, I had some here and there. I had to accept that as we grow older, we must leave space for the new generations. As clients can choose, they will always be attracted to someone younger, which didn't bother me. I've lived through different stages, and each left experiences and satisfactions, and as the years passed, I accepted it and adapted to changes. The only thing that didn't diminish was my independence.

One Saturday, I started my job three times a month as a volunteer at the San Diego Zoo. And once a month at the Wild Animal Park. I passed the first training stage and fell in love with both. The only thing stopping me from going more frequently to the Wild Animal Park was not the park or the type of animals inhabiting there, but the distance— thirty-five minutes away from my condo. And since I tended to drive slowly, I made forty-five.

It was fascinating to spend the weekend surrounded by animals, the noblest creatures on the planet. Although I arrived home tired at the end of the day, the satisfaction of my volunteer work was hugely gratifying.

In the tranquility of my condominium, which I didn't stop remodeling, despite everything being updated, I continued changing decoration, installing a new floor in the garage, and changing kitchen and bathroom furniture. When I had company in the afternoons, we sat down on the patio, where I had a set of chairs and a table with a turquoise blue umbrella. Sipping a glass of wine, we watched the sunset. When I was alone, the glass of wine contributed to my relaxation. Sometimes, I went to have a martini at the happy hour of any restaurant close by.

I kept on traveling with my friends any time the opportunity arose. The friendships from my childhood were still present, and I frequently had visitors from out of town. On the days I had company, I felt like a tourist in my city.

I kept on dancing and participating in competitions but never again bought a four-thousand-dollar dress. And that expensive dress I used at least two times.

My cats became more dependent on me each time. I adored them and gave them a privileged life, to the point of spending 750 dollars in a one-day session with a Pet Psychologist. There was a time when they fought with each other, and I insisted on keeping the peaceful atmosphere they lived under before. I considered it essential to treat them psychologically. And I had the means to do whatever it took for my babys' well-being.

When I reached 76, I believed I had a perfect life with my activities, my independence, and the confidence of a 40-year-old woman. Although, overall, my health was good, I suddenly started having problems with my stomach. Amid my visits to the gastroenterologist and after several treatments that only made me feel worse, seeing that I didn't improve, the doctor ordered a chain of studies and found that I had stomach cancer.

The news made me wobble for some time, but it was just the beginning. I had cancer before, and I managed to overcome it. I knew the side effects of the treatments. It was not fun having to go through them, but inevitably, they were necessary. To me, the important thing was to recover my health and continue with my previous lifestyle— going out to the restaurants I pleased and ordering whatever I felt like. And at 76 years old, I still looked like 60. I was strong and didn't need anyone to do any of my things. My memory was in perfect shape. And I wanted to keep it that way. If possible, until the end of my days.

I started the chemotherapy sessions. Although one of my neighbors insisted on driving me, I never accepted her offer. I went by myself to the oncological clinic and back, knowing that the secondary effects would not start right away, and on the first day, I tried to live normally.

THIRTY

Mariana

The air on that warm morning felt different. The fragrance from the fruit trees in the garden released a smell of stability. The sunshine radiated endlessly. Even the birdsong seemed to welcome me to the new world that, without having planned or thought about it, was already awaiting me.

I woke up in an unknown room. Nevertheless, the familiarity that I experienced in that house made me feel like I had lived there forever. As if the windows and doors, and even the bedspread, had seen me grow up.

It might have been luck or the blood ties that dragged me to that place following the call of my child, or perhaps it was fate willing to reconcile with me to leave behind and try to forget the permanent damage following me— but to have been welcome in such a manner by that couple of extraordinary human beings, seemed inconceivable to me.

In the United States, some people view migrants with a kind eye. They understand the need that most migrants have to find a better job to provide for their families and the effort it takes to cross illegally, sometimes risking their lives, pursuing their vision of the future. But there's another type of people who, without understanding the reasons for an illegal migrant, defend their land where they grew up and feel invaded by migrant groups without stopping to think about their needs. And invariably, they classify them as criminals, fugitives of justice, or drug dealers. With that mentality, they go through life not looking around them and not distinguishing what leads someone to cross the border illegally.

The couple who gave asylum to Gilberto and me are found in the second group, and I ask myself, why did they do it? Then the friendship factor comes up— that tiny seed we plant and water and under our care we see grow, and when it flourishes, it becomes part of the treasures we accumulate to increase the value in the bank of our spiritual bonds.

Mr. and Mrs. Wilson, against their convictions, opened the doors of their house to us and gave us the security of having a roof when we needed it and the well-being sensation that only true friends can provide through difficult times. They welcomed me from the beginning, and not only did I have their unconditional support but a friendship that arose with incommensurate ease from the first day. Being friends with Gilberto for many years before, they never questioned my reasons or opposed our plan— they only supported us without asking for anything in return.

Once solved, at least for some time, the lodging problem, our next step was to focus on rescuing my son. I tried to remain calm, but the minutes and hours seemed eternal. I would've wished to go on the same day we crossed, as I also wanted to ignore Gilberto's plea to wait for some time to avoid any risk. I refused to listen to his advice of not showing up at Carlos Alberto's house first thing the morning after. But we had gone too far in our plan. We had achieved enough to make a false step. We had to act calmly and think smartly before acting. We had to come up with a clever plan.

"Mariana, to show up suddenly at your ex-husband's house won't help us. On the contrary, he knows you can't cross legally. We would need to give him a satisfactory explanation. And even if he allows us to take Ricky with us if he decides to call immigration as we leave, they wouldn't take more than five or ten minutes to locate us and to deport you. NO. We must think before acting."

"I think we can agree if we try to communicate. Carlos Alberto is not mean. He only loses his temper when he drinks or is under the influence of any drug, but if he's sober, you can talk to him, and sometimes he reasons."

"And who tells you we will find him sober when we go?"

"That, I don't know, but it's a risk we must take."

"Wait, I'm thinking about something else."

"Which is?"

"I think it's better if I go alone and talk to him man-to-man. Without losing our tempers or insulting each other. I'll try to make him understand something he seems to forget— the enormous love you feel for Ricky and the need for the child to be with his mom."

"And what if he doesn't agree?"

"Then, will enter plan B. I want that to be our last resource. But, if necessary, I will remind him that we know things about his life and how easy it is to report it to the Navy. He's been doing something illegal for several years, and if he threatens you for having crossed illegally, in the end, he would be the one losing since it would cost him his job. You and I know how important it is to him, and I don't believe he would be willing to take the risk if worse comes to worst."

"I believe you're right. Perchance, this might work. But please, tomorrow, don't let another day pass. I'm desperate to see my son."

"I promise you it will be tomorrow. With luck, we'll be here before lunchtime."

"Mrs. Wilson, I don't know what you're cooking, but it smells good. Can I help to prepare dinner?"

"Under normal circumstances, I would say yes, but tonight, I want to make something special to welcome you. Last night, I only made hot dogs with the intention of you retiring early to rest, but if you like, you can help me to set the table, and if you're patient with my Spanish we can continue communicating. Please correct me if I say something wrong."

"Your Spanish sounds perfect. But I'll be glad to help."

"The weather is pleasant this evening. After dinner, we can sit on the patio and chat for a while to start getting to know each other. And if you like to play cards, perhaps we can play afterward."

"I've never played cards before, but I can learn."

"It's simple and fun. But overall, you need to distract your mind. You have been under indescribable stress over the past few days, and you're in the last weeks of your pregnancy. You need to take care of that tiny creature you're carrying in your womb because, even when you don't believe it, worries can affect your baby. So now, let's eat and chat and play. Agreed?"

"I love the idea."

"Perfect. Dinner is almost ready. Let's only wait until the corn is cooked, and while I finish the salad, my husband will grill the steaks I left marinating. I hope you're not one of those youngsters of today who don't like to eat meat."

"Don't worry, Mrs. Wilson. I eat everything."

"I'm starting to like you already, but please, stop calling me Mrs. Wilson. Let's leave the formalities for a job application. You can call me Nora."

"All right, Nora."

"What would you like to drink? I know what the gentlemen want. But do you want some water, or do you prefer lemonade?

I have a can of concentrate in the freezer. We can prepare it."

"You buy concentrate of lemonade with those gorgeous lemons you have outside? If you allow me, I can cut some and make a pitcher of natural lemonade— the way we make it in Mexico. It only takes sugar and lemon. The key here is to dissolve the sugar in the water first. It tastes delicious because it's all-natural. I assure you it will be to your liking, or if you have agave, we can substitute sugar for agave."

"I don't have agave, but let's try your lemonade with sugar."

= = = = =

"I want to propose a toast to the friendship of many years with Gilberto. And because he has a charming woman by his side. Welcome to our home, and hopefully, all your goals will be met." Mr. Wilson said.

"It is we who want to thank you for your hospitality. Hopefully, we're not being burdensome to you. Tomorrow, once we rescue Ricky, I'll dedicate myself to looking for an apartment or a house, if possible."

"There's no reason to rush looking for a house. There's only Nora and me here, and as you may notice, this house is spacious, so if she agrees, you can stay for as long as you wish, even when the baby is born— by then, maybe, you will find a desired place where you can have your independence."

"I have no problem," Gilberto said, "but I would like to know Mariana's plans."

"Many plans are swirling in my mind. The first one, you know, is to reunite with my son, and once we have him with us, I want to start learning English as soon as possible. I wish to study a technical career, but I don't speak the language and must start learning it. Lastly, now that I'm here, I'd like to locate my family on my father's side."

"I didn't imagine you had family here. I'd love to hear about them, but first, tell me. What kind of career do you have in mind?" Mrs. Wilson asked.

"I've always felt attracted to medicine or psychology. I want to be a nurse assistant. But for now, the priority is to learn English."

"Perhaps you should find out about Community College. In every branch, I believe, they offer ESL, which is English as a Second Language. Once you pass that test, you can study what pleases you."

"Thank you. I will follow your advice and I'm also grateful for your offer to allow us to stay here until the baby's born. If that is the case, in the meantime, I can help you with the house cleaning and, if you wish, in the kitchen."

"It sounds like a great idea, but you must take it easy. I don't want you to take any risk."

"I assure you I won't overdo it. I'll start early in the mornings and stop when I feel tired, but in the meantime, I can be useful."

"While you make that lemonade like the one you prepared tonight, we'll be happy."

"Count on that."

"And now, if you don't mind, can you clarify that about your family? I was under the impression that you had no one else."

"And I have no one but Gilberto and Ricky, but my father, who I never knew was a US citizen of French descent, born and raised here in the USA. All I know is that he died on May 19, 1994. Being a war veteran, it wasn't hard for Gilberto to locate his grave at the Riverside National Cemetery. Maybe someday I could visit his remains. Meanwhile, I know I have a half-sister who must be about my mom's age. She lives in Riverside, and I would like to meet her."

"I'm sorry," interrupted Gilberto. "I don't know if that is a good idea. You know I tried to contact your cousin, the son of your father's brother, who lives in Winchester, and I don't mean to be cruel, but he didn't show interest in knowing you. He was rather concerned about the color of your skin."

"I understand. But keep in mind that we have the same blood. I'm not ruling out the idea of one day meeting my half-sister and knowing if I have nieces or nephews of my age."

"Well," Mr. Wilson said. "There will be time for that. In the meantime, tell us, Gilberto. Have you thought about locations for your mobile home business?"

"Everything happened so suddenly I haven't had a chance. This morning, I was thinking about options. But I am in the same position as Mariana. As soon as we solve Ricky's situation, I will focus immediately on searching for a business place. And, if possible, an apartment or whatever we find not far from the business."

"That's important. Here, the distances can be outrageous, and you two are used to driving short distances with easy traffic. That will be a dramatic change, but you will adapt, eventually."

"I'm sure we will. Thank you again for making us feel at home and for this delicious dinner. Now, if you are ready, we can take advantage of Mariana playing poker while she has no idea how to play. The problem we will have in the future is that she learns with slippery ease."

THIRTY-ONE

Sharing Ricky's custody provoked indescribable anxiety in me. But life, sometimes cruel and sometimes fair, leaned in my favor with my son's full custody. Later than I wished and sooner than I expected, one day not much longer after my San Diego relocation, I had Ricky with me to bring splendor to the years I had left to live.

A bad beginning makes a bad ending. One day, Carlos Alberto's fear turned into reality. They found out about his drug use at his work and took immediate action to fire him. If he had been sinking in the deepness of his swirl, this accelerated his descending. His world was reduced to drugs and nothing else but the uninterrupted use of drugs. With time, he became worse. His body and brain deteriorated until he turned into a mannequin. With no soul, life, hope, or future.

It hurts me deeply to know that the father of my son, the man with whom I shared a brief period of my life, had finished in such a state— and I ask myself, what did I do to deserve the privilege of having escaped at the precise time, to avoid falling and ending up as some of the ones who were part of the group

DOMINANCE DELUSIONS

I once belonged to?

When I left the hospital after my second suicide attempt, I decided that drugs and alcohol abuse or associating with the wrong people interfere with a human being's success. And if one does not get out on time, the day comes when that precise time becomes mistime, and by then, all is lost.

One morning, a couple of months after I crossed to the United States, they found my friend Malú dead in an alley in Tecate. She was ambushed and received several bullets to end up with the execution style. At the age of 28! What pain could surpass that of seeing a life cut short when circumstances didn't even allow her to start living?

The news spread as fire on a strong wind in a city or, should I say, a village where nothing ever happens that gives people a theme to talk about, and when a tragedy of that kind takes place, any small city turns into a village. The press and the rest of the people fuse into one voice, and everyone expresses their opinion, whether they were close or far to the victim, the ones who didn't even know her— everyone finds an unexpected storyline to talk about and takes the opportunity of escaping to their lethal monotony.

I thanked God for having rescued me halfway before sinking into a darkness from which I may not have emerged. Nonetheless, I couldn't avoid suffering the departure of someone so close to me for several years. Although in the end, by taking different paths we grew apart, the affection that kept us together in earlier times, remained there.

I felt oppression in my chest and a sense of guilt for not having done something to rescue my friends in time because Malú was not the only one. Selena continued slowly dying with the excess of drugs and physical abuse by her boyfriend. Those factors came to destroy her and five years later, she couldn't resist either, being in this world to experience more than anything else, that sentiment we all reject named pain. My friends were not guilty of their fate dragging them, and from which I retired wanting to save myself. I left them abandoned to their own devices. Despite Carlos Alberto trying to convince me at that time that none of that was my fault, that each of us chooses the path to follow, he couldn't convince me that he was right.

I feared that Rosita, although rehabilitated from drugs, one day would decide to go back, or even without wanting it, her strength would weaken to end similarly, and that thought, kept me from sleeping at night. I frequently felt anguished about the simplest things. Life scared me. I feared for my friend, my future, and the safety of my children, and the sense of guilt and worry overwhelmed me.

Our routines at Mr. and Mrs. Wilson's house before our little girl's birth had left a path of unforgettable memories. During the day, I tried to help with the house cleaning and in the kitchen. We exchanged recipes. I taught Mrs. Wilson authentic Mexican dishes. She reciprocated by teaching me practical meals I hadn't had before— like meatloaf, mashed potatoes, grilled steaks and hamburgers, baked potatoes, and others. Without realizing it, we became a family. One with a good foundation and close ties, so close they have lasted a lifetime. We enjoyed our afternoons on the patio, drinking lemonade and playing cards. Ricky also wanted to play, and we bought a Monopoly, which the four adults played with him. It excited him to accumulate more properties than anyone else.

All of us were gratified by the warmth of each other's company, and when the time came to move to our place two weeks before our baby's birth, not only did it sadden Mr. and Mrs. Wilson, but we also saw ourselves affected by the separation, luckily the visits from them to our place and ours to theirs became frequent.

DOMINANCE DELUSIONS

If I mentioned before, that I was feeling terrified by the guilt over my friend's death, I must add that for soul illnesses, there's no better cure than time. And as time passed, I gradually adapted to my new life. When our baby girl was born, we named her Cecilia. We all called her Cecy. And with her, the overwhelming happiness of being a mother again was repeated. Having in my arms that tiny creature so helpless, frail, and beautiful, with so much need of protection, convinced me that while she was alive and her parents were still in this world, our mission was to protect her. Soon, we all became familiar with our new home. And the same as with our first place, I put all my enthusiasm into decorating it, although moderately, we focused on the basic needs of the four of us. We had everything we needed and were a happy family.

Our first Christmas together was one of the most beautiful experiences in my life. Cecy was seven months old. She was still a baby to understand the meaning of Christmas. But she knew something unusual was going on each night when the tree saturated with ornaments lit, and seeing all those presents at the bottom, uncontrollable happiness showed on her little face. As for Ricky, he knew well what happened each year on Christmas, and the days to him were eternal, waiting for Santa Claus' arrival.

I had fun buying clothes for Cecy and dressing her as a doll, but in my heart, my two children occupied the same place. Each time I bought something for Cecy, I hurried to the boys' department or a toy store to get something for Ricky. On Christmas Eve, there were as many gifts on the tree as our budget allowed. We delighted at an intimate family dinner, and the day after, Gilberto's children showed up, and there were presents on the tree for them as well. We repeated the family dinner, except on this occasion, there were our two children and the three from Gilberto's previous marriage, his two girls and one boy.

Once Gilberto's children left, we stayed with Ricky, who seemed not to intend to go to bed that evening with that excessive quantity of toys and clothes he received. However, the clothes didn't appeal to him. His excitement centered on the variety of toys he found under the tree. His eyes sparkled with joy, and his happiness was contagious. Gilberto and I could not have asked for more. We had all the good things life could offer us.

If then, we had everything, it didn't take me long to realize that happiness is never complete. Or does it exist? Or is it a utopia? An ephemeral happening that we all need.

Once I thought I had everything, the problems with Fabiola, Gilberto's ex-wife, started. Despite being separated for several years and divorced for six, seeing how happy we were made her realize what she had lost, and it was on her plans to get it back.

Frequently, she threatened to report my illegal cross to the authorities. Tensions arose, and with them, the arguments multiplied, but Gilberto smartly managed the situation until he convinced her that I hadn't done any damage to her, and if things didn't work between them, it wasn't my fault, and now he and I had the right to be happy.

I tried to convince myself that there wasn't a valid reason to worry, but I couldn't find a triumphant explanation that made my fear vanish. And it was my husband who helped me find peace, to make me find comfort in my family, that for as many doubts and insecurities I've been carrying on my shoulders, contemplating my children reminded me that it was my time to be happy, that destiny was in debt with me, that in my life it was them who mattered the most, and, we were all together, knowing that nothing could keep us apart. But again, that's what I decided to think.

THIRTY-TWO

A few months after Cecy's birthday, Gilberto and I opted for legalizing our union with a simple wedding without luxury or splurge. Since my first matrimony, I knew that extravagant weddings representing the fantasy of most women were not for me. Despite both being intimate events, the difference between my first wedding and this one was the actual relationship with my husband, based on respect. The two of us carried some baggage, but the experiences lived and our tenacious desire to avoid failure a second time brought us hope of continuing together through a less rough path.

Each time, I concentrated more on my studies. I established a goal, and the sooner I achieved it, the better. Although I missed that connection with my people and culture, I tried to avoid watching the Spanish channels on television and took advantage of my time watching the channels in English. At first, I struggled to understand, but I didn't want to risk not passing the exam.

The ESL -English as a Second Language- was essential to

advance onto my Certified Nurse Assistant course. I'd had that aspiration since I was a child. I wanted to perform a job through which I could help whoever needed help. I wanted to have a job and a secured check based on doing good deeds and having the satisfaction that, as hard as it might be, at times, knowing that it would be people depending on me to feel better through their harsh moments pushed me to keep going forward.

In my student years, I couldn't make it to advanced studies, and now, going back to school made me feel as if I was trying to reach an unreachable star, but the distance or difficulties to succeed in my goal were not a reason for me to give up. Now, I had my children and wanted them to feel proud of me. I desired to teach them that when we have an objective in mind, we can achieve it no matter how impossible it might seem.

The first thing that came to my mind was to call Gilberto to let him know.

"Gilberto, I'm done."

"And? How did it go?"

"It wasn't bad. I must tell you I would have liked to be among the first ones to finish my test, but, on the contrary, there were only four of us left at the end. It worried me that at any moment, the teacher would say that time was over and we had to leave the classroom. Before I delivered my questionnaire, I wanted to review each question word by word. I don't know if the other three people in the room were in my situation, but I wanted to ensure that not only did I pass the test, but at least 90% of my answers were correct."

"I'm pretty sure it will be that way. When will you have the results?"

"I would like to make you suffer a little and tell you that in two weeks, but you know me. When I have good news to share,

I can't keep it. I PASSED THE EXAM. Do you want me to pick up a pizza? Or do you prefer something else? I hope our little one will be asleep and Ricky awake so that we can celebrate, at least with pizza."

"If I tell Ricky we'll have pizza for dinner, do you think he will go to bed before? He will be awake even if you come at midnight. But don't worry about bringing anything. Your husband already took care of it. And yes! Ricky is awake. We're waiting for you to come home and celebrate. We're proud of you."

The sway of emotions, of fear and joy never stops. At times, it appears there's infinite calm, which produces hope, and when we think the whirlwinds are left behind, unexpected events arise— the peace and comfort of the family, believed to be perfect, are interrupted.

"Gilberto, who were you talking to?"

"It was Fabiola."

"Fabiola, Fabiola, Fabiola! Don't you think that lately, you two have been talking too often?"

"Mariana, please, get those thoughts out of your head. Between Fabiola and I, there's nothing, but we have children together, and sometimes, we need to talk for different reasons."

"It is clear to me that she is the mother of your children. But one thing that is also clear is that she needs you. Not as the father of her children, but as the man she wants by her side and lately more frequently."

"There's no reason to imagine such things. She was only asking me to take her to Home Depot."

"Of course, she wants you to take her to Home Depot. On Monday, she wanted you to bring her some things from the pharmacy. And yesterday to help her fill out a form. And tomorrow, what shall she need?"

"I don't know, Mariana. But I can't turn my back on her."

"And I'm not asking you to do it when she needs you, but you know she's only looking for excuses for you to see her every day."

"Is not every day."

"Not every day, but often enough for you to make her understand that now you have a family, and therefore, a responsibility with your wife and children here."

"I think you're overreacting. I'll try to speak to her. I assure you, there's no reason to worry."

"I would like to think that way."

"Oh, it's you. You didn't tell me you were not coming to dinner."

"I'm sorry. I didn't realize how time flew by. My oldest daughter had a volleyball game. You know how hungry teenagers are after a game. I took them to eat hamburgers. We got involved in a conversation, and they were having a good time. I couldn't tell them I had to leave."

"I suppose Fabiola was also having a good time. But it's late, and I'm not in the mood to argue. I'm going to bed."

= = = = =

"Mariana, what are these suitcases doing in the living room?"

"They are mine and the children's things."

"Where are you going?"

"Moving to Tecate."

"What do you mean, moving to Tecate?"

"That's the only option I see to save our marriage before the ship sinks."

"Why are you mentioning a sinking ship? We have a good marriage. It's all well."

"You are well. The children and I are not. You decide. You can come with us. Or you stay here and run to Fabiola every time she snaps her fingers."

"You know I love you with all my heart. If I've been acting wrong, I didn't realize how much it affected you. You and the children are my priority, but I also want to be a fit father for my other children."

"I'm not asking you not to fulfill your obligations with your other family, but I'm not willing to continue tolerating this situation. You either come with us or stay here to start a new life with Fabiola and your other children."

"I have no doubts about spending the rest of my days with you, Ricky, and Cecy, but please, could you give me a couple of days to see what I will do with my business?"

"You have always succeeded in everything you start, let alone in Tecate, where you have a virgin market and know so many people, and so many know you."

THIRTY-THREE

Four years of contemplating the immensity of a blue sky, the starry nights, the tranquility of a small city where everyone knows each other, reconnecting me with my culture, eating the food I liked, and enjoying my family's harmony to the fullest, increased my wealth of spirit— but our children were growing up and, we needed to think about their studies and their future.

Living in Tecate allowed us a quiet life for a few years, and it was time to return to the United States, except that this time, under different circumstances, doubtless and fearless, our family was solid, despite Fabiola never giving up and continued interfering to interrupt the happiness between Gilberto and I. But I needed to focus again on what had always been my objective— to be a certified nurse assistant or to study any other technical career related to medicine or patient care and to give Gilberto the opportunity to start a business to secure our financial future and our children's education.

I also prayed that by returning to the United States, I wouldn't be jeopardizing our marriage stability.

DOMINANCE DELUSIONS

"Gilberto, I'm a loser. I don't know why I have been deluded by this idea, knowing I don't have studies. I don't have the intelligence to make it."

The sobs overwhelmed me. I felt defeated— my hopes started to vanish, and sadly, now they seemed more distant than ever.

"Calm down, Mariana. Why do you say that? If someone has determination, it is you. And your intelligence is astonishing. Did something happen with your exam, and you didn't pass it? If it's that, let me remind you, when you took that exam for English and mathematics, you thought it would be a piece of cake, and it wasn't. However, you didn't give up. It wasn't until the second time that you passed it."

"Yes. You're right. It's only that I was so excited about passing this admission test to start studying as soon as possible, but things happen for a reason. I will try once more, and next time will be easier. I remember the questions in the exam, and I'm not planning on failing again."

Eight years later

"Mariana, how would you like to take a trip? You and me alone."

"I don't know if that would work."

"It is something that the two of us need. We had gone through countless hard times with Cecy's situation. It's unbelievable how today's young people stagger as they become teenagers. And how easily they follow others' wrong patterns to fall into depression for no apparent reason."

"That's right. No one more than you knows the pain I've been dragging through my life, but none had been superior to the thought of not being wise enough to help our daughter."

"I admit you did the unimaginable to rescue our Cecy from

the state of depression in which she found herself."

"I believe it helped me to personally have suffered depression, to identify her behavior in time."

"And you succeeded with your timely intervention. Let's make that trip I'm suggesting. You choose the destination."

"But at this point in our lives, do you see any benefit in this trip? I see it hard that you could change. Each day, you become more jealous and controlling. I think you have always seen me as the daughter you want to discipline, not as the wife who needs you, as a lover who, in the full bloom of youth, needs a man by her side, a true partner."

"I know we've been having problems lately, and believe me, I would do anything to avoid them, but you must understand that I'm 62 years old. And you are 42 and look like 32. I can't stop being jealous. Don't think the way men look at you is unnoticeable."

"So what if men look at me? I only have eyes for you, and I have always proved it. Where does this insecurity suddenly come from? But it's not only that. The monotony is to blame. It's starting to wear me out. If it were up to you, you would not even let me work, and I need to do something with my life. I need to feel useful. You know how I love my work. Most importantly, you should know that I've never been unfaithful. Between the monotony and your jealousy, we're growing apart instead of getting closer."

"Please don't say that. I don't want to know we're growing apart."

"But we are."

"I have faith that things could change with time."

"I hope so. You and I have been through countless things together. I'd probably feel lost without you, but I don't see a way out except for a separation."

= = = = =

DOMINANCE DELUSIONS

For several years, this road had been familiar. Since Gilberto and I kept our property in Tecate, I come to this town frequently, but today, it felt different. When I remember Carlos Alberto's mother, I relate her to pain and associate her with bad moments, but first, people change with time. Second, years ago, I decided to live a lighter life and learned to forget and forgive.

I could not believe it when my former mother-in-law wanted to see Ricky and me. I knew she was sick. I didn't know that she was on her last days, though. She said what she needed, and I did the same with her. Undoubtedly, life is full of surprises.

I was under the impression that Carlos Alberto stopped living years back when he sank as low as he did with drugs, but faith attracts miracles. He converted to Christianity and left drugs and alcohol for good. He was reborn to straighten his life. From what I noticed through our conversation with his mother, she was also influenced by her son's faith. It was a relief to see the turn of events in such an unexpected way.

THIRTY-FOUR

I refuse to accept how time flies. We don't even feel it, and it doesn't allow us a moment of reflection, of going back to the happy memories and to be able to caress them in our minds, making some time to relive them, or to remember the unhappy circumstances and to appreciate the victory of having overcome them.

Today, I want to defy time and say a prayer for the treasures accumulated in my life— for one, to have obtained that license to work on what I've always wanted, and for two, to have sufficient experience to start a caregiver business and feel I can continue with my target of helping all the people who need my help through my job.

Now that I have all the permits and requirements for my business, I wish to continue with my plans. I see my children, and the blissfulness wraps me up all over when I see Ricky with the countless qualities that make him the perfect candidate for any woman— a handsome young man, athletic, hard-working, and responsible he has become at the age of 25, but above all, teaming up with his father to help him in his garden lighting company, gives me, and his dad, enormous peace of mind.

Gilberto never doubted when the opportunity knocked to open that type of business. I was skeptical at the beginning about the radical change. But Gilberto is also a hard worker and fully dedicated, and it didn't take him long to realize this was the type of business he would be in until the day of his retirement.

As to my marriage, although we're both going through a painful time, there's a moment when weariness defeats us, and we must learn when things have come to an end. I was hopeful we could take couples therapy and save what we were trying to prevent from continuing to deteriorate. Unfortunately, in our Latino culture, men don't accept talking about a couple's problems to someone unknown outside the family. Except for rare exceptions, most men don't agree with taking that step as an alternative to improving the couple's situation.

I remember my first divorce and the immense peace I felt having walked away from the man who only caused me uneasiness. I was also terrified of ending up alone, being part of a group of divorced women. But this time, after twenty years of marriage, it pleases me to know the story won't repeat. I'm not afraid of loneliness.

I must thank life for hitting me everywhere from every angle and in so many different ways that made me similar to those inflatable dummies with weights at the bottom, making it impossible to bring them down, and thanks to that, I learned to be strong since childhood.

I lived happily with Gilberto for many years, and from him, I learned endless things unknown to me. I wish our stability, love, and trust in each other had lasted a lifetime, but nothing is eternal. When misfortune knocks on our door, we must open it to focus on finding solutions for our future. Hiding to avoid unexpected situations is like trying to swim against the current.

This is the time in my life to plan and look forward to a

hopeful future while life continues. I love my job. It gives me endless satisfaction to know I'm doing better each day, no matter how busy I can be, and I don't discard the idea of attending the university to increase my nursery knowledge.

Cecy and I long for that trip to Germany and other European countries, and we hope to make it soon. This time, it will be just the two of us. The idea of making that trip together excites us. As for Ricky, the time also came for a change in his life. He moved out of the house to share an apartment with his girlfriend, and like many young couples, they are happy with each other's company. I don't see him as frequently as I would like because my job takes most of my time, and we live in different areas, not that close to each other, but we speak frequently, and the bond between him and I remains indestructible.

Gilberto left a long path of good memories in my life. Cecy made me stagger as she entered adolescence in those moments when, like many other young people, depression takes over them. But our Cecy was worth too much for the three of us in the family to allow her to sink into that sad illness that many teenagers succumb without hope. I'm grateful to this life for sending me the signal at that precise moment and, as a mother, allowing me to fight against all odds to rescue my daughter. Now, at sixteen years old, she is a beautiful girl with a bright future. How fortunate we all were! To have been able to help her and with her, to reinforce that unity that, above all, was the pillar of our family.

Nonetheless, things took a different direction between Gilberto and me, and the only solution we found for our lives was to divorce, neither he nor I know what the future has in store for us.

THIRTY-FIVE

Katya

It was time to cut ties with Denver. I left behind fond memories that will always stay with me. The same goes for my friends to whom distance doesn't exist. It took me a while to come to this decision. But I finally thought that my best option was to sell those two rental properties I've kept for all those years. It pleased me to know I had a secure monthly income, but being realistic, money was the only thing I had in abundance. My income covered my lifestyle. And if I was sure about something, it was about not moving from La Jolla. I would spend the rest of my days here. I lived happily in my condo, and if the sale of the two properties in Denver allowed me a new investment, this would be in La Jolla or somewhere near this area.

I planned a trip to Denver to see what I had in my storage and decide what to bring back. I'd always been a practical woman. But I found it hard to detach from certain material things, like the furniture. And I was sure that by bringing them to La Jolla, the only thing I would be doing would be to transfer them from one storage to the other. My condominium was decorated to my liking, and the antique furniture I had kept for that long didn't fit within my contemporary style. However, I couldn't let them go. I would try my best to sell some things, and the ones with the highest sentimental value would return with me. It was decided!

I still didn't understand why I let them convince me to visit that retirement home. The place was incredible. Perhaps what attracted me the most was that fancy building and their everyday activities to make the residents there think that they are on permanent vacation in a five-star hotel. I could imagine myself every afternoon with a martini in my hand, listening to the piano player, and after savoring a superb dinner, choosing between playing cards or any other game or watching a movie on the gigantic screen of the playroom, but what I didn't imagine, is that to reserve one of their units, they asked for a million-dollar deposit.

Ha! As if I needed someone to prepare me an exquisite dinner, there was a large variety of restaurants in this area, and I could choose whatever pleased me. Sitting alone at a bar and ordering a martini didn't intimidate me. I still liked and could cook whatever I felt like, and there was always a friend who wanted to play cards or go to the movies with me. The only thing I didn't have was that ridiculous one-million-dollar deposit because neither the money from the sale of my Denver properties nor the one I would receive from the one in Las Vegas could be enough, or maybe it would. But I still had several years of independent life before I started thinking about such an extravagance.

DOMINANCE DELUSIONS

I didn't know what was going on with my Vegas property. It seemed suspicious that it hadn't been sold after being on the market for one month, and the weirdest thing was that a former co-worker from the real estate agency who lived on the same street where my house was, told me that she had noticed some night activity. I didn't know what kind of night activity she referred to, and she was not sure either, but soon, I would find out.

I mistakenly told my neighbor about my plan to travel to Vegas at the beginning of the following week. The moment I mentioned going alone and driving, she scolded me as no one had since I was seven years old and focused all her energy trying to persuade me from that road trip— what if the dangers of the road, what if the heat, what if the distance...How little did she know me! I would leave on Tuesday the following week. Her only concern should be not to see any strange activity during my absence and that the cat sitter would show up at the agreed time to take care of my babies.

For three consecutive days in Vegas, I went at different hours during the night, and I didn't see any activity. I shouldn't have told my real estate agent that I was there. The one with the nocturnal activity was her since she was the only one with a key. The good thing was that I showed up at the office and asked to see her marketing plan. I would have been surprised if under that pressure, my house would have lasted more than two weeks in the market without selling.

Seeing things through my pink prism, I took the opportunity to see Celine Dion in concert. One of my Vegas friends went with me to the show, and the morning after, we had brunch.

That time, I let her choose. I was sure she would pick the best in Vegas, and on Sunday morning, I left almost at dawn to beat the heat.

= = = = =

Fourteen months after selling my last property outside La Jolla, I tried to live normally, but my stomach started bothering me again. The list of things I could eat was limited. I recognized the signal. For the third time, cancer had visited me.

The chemotherapies before had different side effects. On this occasion, I only felt an insufferable tiredness that prevented me from getting out of bed, but same as last time, the first two days, I felt normal, and I continued with my routine.

If I was never in a state of shock from the chemotherapies, my neighbor who consistently worried about me was. One day, when she saw me washing my garage floor after returning from chemotherapy, she was close to snatching the broom from my hand and hitting me with it.

"What are you doing, woman? Didn't you have chemo today?"

"Yes, and I'm back."

"That, to me, is clear as a bell. But why aren't you resting, as you should be?"

"Because my body hasn't asked me to rest. I assure you that as soon as it does, I will."

"But washing the garage floor? When you keep this place impeccable all the time?"

"I had workers yesterday going in and out as they pleased. Trust me. I will feel better today with my garage clean."

"All right, all right. I know I won't win this one. Let me know if you need anything."

After finishing chemotherapy, I had a brief recess, and later, I continued with the radiation marathon. Thirty sessions and I didn't feel any improvement. The doctor tried to convince me they were necessary to be sure there was no metastasis and that my body was cancer-free.

During my treatments, I turned 80, and on my birthday, I received a shower of life appreciation. I realized how loved I was not only by my family but also by the number of friends I had, some of them from my childhood, as was the case of Sandy, and others from my student days. Regardless of how old the friendships were, they all survived time and distance. My sister came to visit and celebrate with me. Although we could not do the celebration we would have liked, the doctor gave me a week's break, and my sister, a friend, and I took a night boat tour to the San Diego Bay.

Because of my long treatment, my sister had to return to Missouri to take care of personal matters. Things kept on complicating. I hadn't finished radiation when COVID-19 hit. And, on the days I felt like going out to dinner or somewhere else, I preferred to stay at home for fear of getting infected.

As soon as the vaccine became available, I had my first shot, then a second one, and a booster, but even with all the precautions, I couldn't escape this highly contagious disease. My symptoms, I didn't wish to anyone, but I consider myself lucky. They were not the kind that sent people to the hospital fighting for their lives with artificial respirators.

I hadn't finished my round of radiation therapies when I had to interrupt the treatment. Suddenly, I felt worse than ever. I checked into the hospital, where I remained for five days. I missed my babies, Louis and Louise, but I left them in good hands with the pet sitter, who, by then, knew the routine and had the keys to my place so she could go as needed.

My two bits of tenderness spent most of the time in the window waiting to see me return. I couldn't bear the idea, but flipping the coin, I felt privileged in the hospital. They assigned me a two-corner room that made me feel like I was in a presidential suite with a phenomenal panoramic view. All the staff pampered me, and my room could've been taken for a flower shop. We were amid the pandemic, and people didn't want to get close to hospitals. Floral arrangements replaced personal visits.

After five days, I left the hospital, only for a short time since, from then on, the game of checking in and out of the hospital became frequent. Sometimes, I drove, and other times, the ambulance came to pick me up. They continued performing all types of studies— I don't know for what reason. I believe the results were already written.

The regimen of a strict diet began. The list of things I could eat was reduced each time. Three days after Christmas, I ended up in the hospital again. On December 30th, I was released with the doctor's blessing, allowing me to eat whatever I wanted on New Year's Eve. We spent it in the house— Louis, Louise, and me. For them, I went to a gourmet pet store and bought everything I found that caught my eye. And for me, I stopped by a seafood restaurant and ordered lobster and oysters Rockefeller to go. I also had a glass of wine with dinner, considering it would be my last supper.

The day after, I checked into the hospital for the last time and spent forty-eight hours there. And the rest, Mariana, is history. The day that not only you but the other caregivers came to this place, was between my trips to the hospital. When they sent me home, they suggested I should have full-time caregivers to feed me through these tubes. And to do everything else you already know.

THIRTY-SIX

"Doctor Reynolds, will I go this week to take care of Mrs. Katya?"

"Mariana, thank you for reminding me. Her family had been calling over the weekend. I promised them to send you on Monday as soon as you came."

"Did you say her family? I didn't know she had family here."

"Different people have been calling. The first identified herself as the patient's sister— later, a niece called, and lastly, a gentleman who said he was her brother. It seems they have a full house. And Mrs. Katya insists on you going."

"Then, if you don't need anything else, I'll go there now."

"Thank you for reminding me. We've been short on staff and extremely busy with the fire at the retirement home. How sad! A true unfortunate happening."

"It's a shame that something like this happened. Let me know if you need me to work overtime. I will call you before my shift is over."

"Please, do so. If, as you said, you're willing to do it, you might need to work a double shift. I don't want to be a pessimist, but it is not a good sign that the entire family is at Mrs. Katya's. Perhaps she might be living her last days or hours. You might not even finish your shift with her today."

"Probably. But her strength is stunning. At 81 years old, with a three-times recurring cancer. With the type of surgery she recently had, her chemotherapies' marathon, and being a COVID survivor. We never know how far someone can get with the cling-to-life desire."

"Mariana, thank God you're already here. Katya has been asking for you. She had called each of us to say goodbye."

"To say goodbye?"

"Yes. The doctor said she probably, wouldn't make it through the night. Perhaps it's just a matter of hours. For the past five days, she hasn't received anything but water, same, that comes out through one of the tubes attached to her body."

"How painful it is to see her like that."

"It is painful for us, the family, and the people who love her, but she's not suffering. She's fighting until her last breath and ready to leave when her heart stops beating."

"Mariana, come close. Sit down next to my bed."

"I'm here, Katya."

Taking Katya's hand in hers, Mariana, with a warm look and the bond created among them in the past weeks, tried to transmit safety to her patient while this clung to the hand of her caregiver, as a child holds his father's hand to avoid a fall into a canyon.

"Do you see that picture on top of the dresser? I would like you to keep it. We didn't have time to talk about it. We talked about most of my trips, but this was from the last time I traveled to Africa, my favorite of all the ones I could've done. You know how much I love animals and that closeness to them and nature. It made me feel my life was worth living. Maybe one day you can frame it, and it will remind you of one of the most beautiful sunsets this planet gave me. And look at that giraffe, squandering freedom in a land created for them, and that sometimes, we humans end up destroying."

"Thank you, Katya. I promise you to frame it, and through that gorgeous sunset, I will always remember you."

"It was a beautiful and expensive trip. But please, don't be dazzled by that blinding shine you never saw, by the life I lived and that you never experienced, because destiny is written for each of us. I had much of what you lacked, but now you have something I don't have— TIME and YOUTH, the most precious gifts humans don't appreciate. Hold on to them while you can, and if you add those gifts to your family, you will realize how fortunate you are. You were blessed with those children you adore, and I'm sure they adore you the same way. Together, you can defy the world and overcome any obstacle in life. Don't ever forget this— a family is the most valuable treasure you can possess. It's like a plant that we must water every day, and when we see that one of its leaves or flowers starts browning, with care and dedication, we can make it healthy again."

Mariana listened carefully to these words, and when she realized Katya's labored breathing, she asked her to relax for a moment.

"I'm here, Katya. I'm not going anywhere." She said, squeezing her patient's hand while she felt it loosen to her last breath until she became motionless in that bed that kept her prisoner for the last days of her existence.

With her hand, Mariana gently closed Katya's eyes and left the room to call the family and tell them her patient was gone.

"Blessed be the Lord." Her brother said. "Katya lived a privileged life. But even privileges have an expiration date. She was ready to leave — since last night, she had been talking with each family member. And she had time to say goodbye to all of us. She was in good spirits, showing once more how brave she was. She lived life to the fullest with amazing strength. She enjoyed her past, her present, and even the future she imagined. She was an intelligent woman, and when she realized that there was no future on the horizon, she accepted her destiny with resignation and gave all of us who love her the acceptance of the inevitable end."

Mariana grabbed her coat and her purse and said goodbye to the family, to leave suddenly. The winter breeze, damping her face, disguised a silent tear rolling down her cheek. For some time, she remained in her car, looking at the picture given to her, reliving that beautiful sunset and trying to understand at what point a close friendship developed between that woman from a different world, who was about 40 years older than her but in the end, neither age nor the accumulated experiences could avoid that closeness that seldom happens in life.

Grabbing her mobile phone, she called her office and informed them that her services were no longer needed at Katya's home and that she was ready for her next shift. With her sight lost, looking without seeing anything in particular, with shaky hands contemplating the photograph, she turned her face to see Katya's house one last time. It was the moment to leave. But once she left that place, it would be the end. She turned again to look at the house, at the window where Louis and Louise awaited who knows what because they were also aware of the emptiness and absence. Although soon, their new home would be in Missouri, many miles from San Diego, they wanted to remain in that window where they saw their mom carrying all those bags of goodies for them, their mom, with a happy heart and hope that life brings along.

= = = = =

Mariana starts her car and advances a few steps to the intersection, where she sees that vehicle coming in the opposite direction— the equipment inside is familiar as it is the number of people there and what their duty will be upon arrival to their destination and also what they would transport in the silence of that cold Winter afternoon at the beginning of the year 2022.

We, authors, owe our success
to our readers' reviews.
If you enjoyed this book,
please consider writing
an honest review on Amazon.

Thank you for reading

DOMINANCE DELUSIONS.

Other books by Alma Lazar

Delirios de Dominio
When the Light Goes Out
Cuando la Luz se Apaga

www.almalazar.com
Instagram: @authoralmalazar

Made in the USA
Las Vegas, NV
09 April 2025